To James

In the hope you may

Read a Book !! ?


David
2011

Wolves have been despised and persecuted by humans for centuries. They were eradicated completely in England by about 1509 and in Scotland and Ireland in the mid-eighteenth century. Yet superstitions and folklore continue to fuel a fear of wolves in modern day Britain – even though many of these popular beliefs are inaccurate. In *Howls of Imagination* Dr Paul Williams describes how these beliefs have arisen, and contrasts them with known information about wolves – and the relatively rare number of wolf attacks on humans.

Why did Christian allegories give wolves a 'bad press'? How did popular literature breed a hybrid lore by mixing legends about real wolves with myths about werewolves? Have children really been reared by wolves? And, above all, should we afraid of 'the big bad wolf' or simply consign such ideas to the scrap bin of erroneous stereotypes? *Howls of Imagination* reveals how folklore and myth can create and sustain misleading ideas while simultaneously offering a more factual understanding of this iconic animal of the wilderness.

**Dr Paul Williams** completed a PhD thesis on wolves in folklore in 2004 at Sheffield University. His short fiction and poetry has been published in magazines and anthologies such as *Focus* and *Roadworks.*

# Howls of Imagination

## Wolves of England

## Paul Williams

**Heart of Albion**

**Howls of Imagination: Wolves of England**

**Paul Williams**

Cover illustration by Ian Brown

ISBN 978-1-872883-98-2

Published by

**Heart of Albion Press**
2 Cross Hill Close, Wymeswold
Loughborough, LE12 6UJ

albion@indigogroup.co.uk

**Visit our Web site: www.hoap.co.uk**

Printed in England by Booksprint

# Contents

# Introduction

# Do wolves eat humans?

Wolves have been despised and persecuted by humans for centuries. Reasons for this hatred include a fear of competition for prey, a desire to protect livestock and a belief that wolves eat people, especially children. This last belief is recorded in folklore, oral traditions and historical records of many cultures. It is not supported by modern statistics or historical research.

In 2002 the belief in wolves eating humans was challenged when a team of researchers, led by John Linnell, published a study of wolf attacks on humans (Linnell 2002). Evidence for the global study was taken from historical records, newspapers and oral testimony, dating back to the sixteenth century. The researchers concluded that the majority of fatal attacks were made by rabid wolves. Rabies was once commonplace in Europe and North America, being transmitted from animals to humans with fatal consequences. The disease causes insanity in its victims, causing them to act abnormally. If most wolf attacks on humans can be attributed to rabies then it suggests that attacking humans is not normal wolf behaviour.

In the period between 1952 and 2002 Linnell's team found seventeen instances in Europe and Russia in which wolves had killed people and none in North America. Most reports of wolf attacks in the period covered by the study came from pre-twentieth century France, Estonia and northern Italy. They were placed in three categories – attacks by rabid animals, predatory attacks (usually on children), and defensive, the latter where humans had provoked the wolf.

The incidents of predatory attacks in the twentieth century were:

   ♦   5 children killed in Poland in 1937.

   ♦   4 children killed in Spain between 1957 and 1974.

   ♦   36 children killed in Russia between 1944 and 1953.

   ♦   273 children killed in India.

This is a total of 318. In the twentieth century brown and grizzly bears killed 313 people, tigers several thousand, lions 303 and leopards 336 (Linnell 2002: 35) Other statistics show that domestic dogs bite an estimated 1 million people in the United States each year with sixteen to eighteen percent of those victims dying (Linnell

2002: 32). In a five year period in the Indian state of Madhya Pradesh 735 people were attacked by sloth bears, 138 by leopards, 121 by tigers, 34 by elephants, 29 by wild boar, 21 by guar, 13 by wolves and three by hyenas (Linnell 2002:38). Linnell commented that wolves were among the least dangerous of all wildlife species. This conclusion has not always been supported by the consensus of public opinion.

## Scientific evidence

The conclusions of Linnell's team endorse the observations of scientists who have observed wolves in the wild and described them as timid and eager to avoid humans. Scientific study of the wolf began in 1944 with the publication of Adolph Murie's research into the ecology of Mount McKinley National Park in Alaska. Murie was the first person to examine wolves in their natural habitat and report objectively on these observations. He challenged the longstanding belief in wolves as natural predators on people but his ideas were not widely disseminated outside of the scientific community.

In 1970 David Mech published *The Wolf: the ecology and behaviour of an endangered species,* which remains the definitive guide. Drawing mainly on his own observations in North America, he described wolves as elusive creatures that were afraid of people. He helped persuade people there were errors in common perceptions of wolves, especially in North America. He also helped unite wolf researchers around the world. The results of studies conducted by these researchers are no longer confined to scientific texts but have been made available to the public on the internet and in television documentaries. Almost all of them support the conclusions of Mech and Murie. Why then were wolves hated by humans for so long?

## Superstition

Wolves tend to hide from people. This is understandable as they are often hunted. Their elusiveness has helped humans construct myths around them. In previous times wolves lived outside human society in dark woods where people rarely went. Those woods filled gaps between villages and were largely avoided. They were also home to other wild animals, outlaws and criminals. The term 'wolfs-head' denotes an outlaw in the laws of Edward the Confessor and was used in this context for several centuries afterwards.

Most of the 'wild woods' in England were actively managed by the end of the Anglo-Saxon period but they were still feared until an industrialized society took control of them. One idea which occurs repeatedly in human history is the perceived necessity of taming, or controlling, the wilderness. Classical mythology describes numerous unpleasant monsters that were thought to live in wild places. English translations of the Bible from the fourteenth century onwards stressed the negative connotations of the wilderness. One writer counted 245 references to the wilderness in the Old Testament and thirteen in the New Testament, not including the usage of terms such as wasteland and desert. (Nash 1967 (1973: 13)). Now that the world has been fully explored these places are not feared as much as they once were but previously in their preferred forest habitat wolves became associated with evil. Stories of wolf attacks on people reinforced this connotation.

Other animals such as the mountain gorilla and giant panda were assumed to be hostile to humans before they were officially discovered. Scientists demonstrated that these impressions were incorrect and they were quickly discarded. Popular beliefs about wolves have also been challenged by scientists but, as yet, have not been removed. Part of this is due to their longevity. Wolves have been a part of European folklore for much longer than the panda or gorilla and consequently beliefs about them are harder to dislodge, if they are indeed false.

### The wolf today

In 1999 there were an estimated 150,000 wolves in 41 countries around the world (Route and Aylesworth 1999). Wolves were eradicated completely in England by *circa* 1509, Scotland *circa* 1743, Ireland *circa* 1776, Japan *circa* 1910 and France *circa* 1920 (although some wolves have now returned to France). Wolves currently occupy just five percent of the territory they formerly roamed in the United States and have been eliminated from fifteen of the twenty-three European countries where they were once common. The main explanation for this is hunting.

### Reasons why wolves are hunted

The three main motivations for hunting are profit, fear of competition and the urge to kill. A fourth, of no relevance to wolves, is the desire for food. Fear of disease is a possible fifth reason, although the spreading of disease through animals was not always recognised.

Profit is not a significant motivation for the destruction of wolves. The high prestige attached to wolf skins offers some reward to poachers but generally they can find richer, and easier, pickings elsewhere as the wolf's skin is too brittle to possess any real commercial value in the clothing industry. I saw wolf skins on sale in the department stores of Ulaan Baatar, Mongolia, in 2003 for sixty dollars which is a small amount compared to the cost of other animal skins. In most cases wolves are hunted for sport and because they are considered to be a threat to people and livestock.

### Wolf predation on animals

In 1800 Delabere Blaine wrote a hunting treatise which was extremely hostile towards wolves. After describing wolf hunting in Germany, India and Russia he stated: 'We hardly need a plea for the propriety of introducing wolf hunting in Britain when it is notorious that the ravages of this animal proved very destructive, not only to the animals around him, but also on many occasions, to the human inhabitants, children we are told were sought for by him and fell a prey to his thirst for blood.' (Blaine 1800 (1852: 104–5)). It is unclear why Blaine is advocating wolf hunting in a country where wolves no longer existed in the wild.

According to Blaine, wolves in Livonia, the former Polish territory now split between Latvia and Estonia, killed the following numbers of animals in 1823:

- 15,182 sheep

- 4,190 swine

- 2,544 goats

- 1,867 horned cattle

- 1,841 horses

- 1,243 foals

- 733 calves

- 726 lambs

- 705 dogs

- 673 geese

- 312 suckling pigs

- 183 kids

    (Blaine 1840 (1852: 78))

We do not know where Blaine obtained these figures from or how they were calculated. *The Times* quotes an appendix to a report, published in St Petersburg in 1876, which said that: in one province in 1873 40,000 cattle were killed by wolves. (*The Times*, 8 August 1876: 6) It goes on to state that the estimated 170,000 wolves in Russia killed around 200 million feathered game per annum. It also stated that wolf predation accounted for the loss of more cattle than pestilence and fire. A report later in the same newspaper claimed that 200,000 wolves in European Russia in 1875 killed 108,000 cattle plus poultry and dogs. (*The Times* 21 June 1877: 5)

These figures contrast sharply with modern statistics. In north-west Montana in 2001 wolves were responsible for one percent of cattle and four percent of sheep killed by predators (Alliance for the Wild Rockies 2006). On average wolves in central Idaho kill four cattle, eighteen sheep and one dog each year (Paul 2006). Wolves in the Yellowstone National Park are responsible for killing seven cattle, 25 sheep and one dog each year (Paul 2006).

Mech contended that a wolf eats an average of 132 pounds of meat each day (Mech 1962: 77). Another researcher estimated they need 175 pounds of meat each per day (Lopez 1978: 54). Blaine's figures only relate to domestic animals and do not include wild prey so one must assume that either his statistics, or the wolf population of Livonia at that time, were unduly high.

Some governments now pay farmers for loss of livestock to wolves, firstly because they are obliged to comply with European directives that promote sustainable populations of large carnivores and, secondly, because they are realising that wolves attract tourists. The compensation offers have led to a number of false claims. In relation to compensation package in Italy Erik Zimen and Luigi Boitani estimated, from information supplied by national park superintendents and other authorities that less than half the reported damages were actually caused by wolves (Zimen and Boitani 1979: 61). Zimen also described a fraud in which sheep were killed by farmers in order to claim the compensation (Zimen 1981: 276–7). One American scientist investigated 100 cases of animals supposedly killed by wolves and discovered that wolves were responsible for just five of the casualties (MacIntyre 1995: 53). People sometimes lie about the wolf when they have something to gain.

**Contradictions**

The image of the wolf presented by modern scientists and in Linnell's report contrasts with widely held beliefs. This book will examine attitudes towards wolves, concentrating on beliefs about wolves attacking people in England. Wolves have not roamed freely through the English countryside for at least three hundred years although they can be seen in zoos and safari parks. In 2001 sixteen private individuals residing in England had a license to keep wolves (*Wolves* 2 (2002): 7). For the majority of people opinions and attitudes towards wolves are shaped, not by personal observation, but by art and the media.

Between June 1999 and December 2001 I conducted a survey on contemporary attitudes towards wolves in England. 187 people replied. Some of their answers will be considered in this book, putting each question into a historical context. To understand how perceptions of wolves developed in England let us begin by examining the history of wolves in the country.

# Chapter one

# History of the wolf in England

We know that wolves once existed in England because of prehistoric remains and occasional references in literature and documents. Skulls and teeth of ancient wolves found in various locations are in museums and private collections. Archaeological evidence indicates a widespread distribution throughout the country with bones discovered in Berkshire, Derbyshire, Devon, Essex, Gloucestershire, Lancashire, Kent, Norfolk, Oxfordshire, Somerset, Sussex, Wiltshire and Yorkshire. Wolves are keen travellers and presumably roamed the whole country. Modern research has identified individual wolves in north-west America that travelled more than eight hundred kilometres (Fritts 1983: 166–7).

Sources from Saxon and Norman times do not indicate the existence of a widespread hostility towards wolves. Saxon personal names such as Eadwulf ('noble wolf'), Berthwulf ('industrious wolf'), Ealdwulf ('old wolf'), Byrthwulf ('bright wolf') and others indicate a certain respect for wolves. In the first volume of *English Historical Documents*, edited by Dorothy Whitelock, there are eighty-two charters, grants of property and other legal documents from 672 to 1036 in which the names of signatories and others mentioned are compounds of 'Wulf'.

Such names belong consistently to people of a higher rank and none of the people mentioned from the lower ranks had Wulf in their name. There are also Saxon place-names featuring the term Wulf; these too could indicate respect. Wolf derivatives also appear in town names. Wolverton in Buckinghamshire, Woolverton in Somerset and Wolferton in Norfolk come from the Old English personal name Wulfhere. Wolverhampton, which has a football team nicknamed the Wolves, was named after Lady Wulfrana in AD 985 and literally means 'Wulfrana's settlement on the hill'.

## Mediaeval wolf hunters

In the forest laws of Canute of 1016 the wolf, along with the fox, was referred to as neither a beast of the forest nor of venery. This meant they were not protected from hunters, although anyone killing them within a royal forest would be liable to pay compensation. Animals on royal land were there for royals and their friends to hunt. A law passed by Henry I in the early twelfth century granted compensation for anyone injured during a wolf-hunt. It seems that wolves were hunted for sport, rather than with the intention of eliminating them. This suggests that wolves were not considered unduly dangerous to people or livestock. If they had been a major threat, hunting would have been more intense. Later the wolf was considered to be a beast of venery in some counties at least, as shown in a hunting treatise entitled the *Book of St Albans*, first published in 1486.

The first evidence of organised wolf hunting, ignoring sport, appears during the thirteenth century when some noblemen were given land in return for driving away wolves and other predators. These included Vitalis Engaine in 1242 and Sir John d'Engayne in 1275, both in the county of Northamptonshire. Others, such as John Giffard in 1280, were given a free rein to kill wolves in all parts of the realm. The most widely quoted document was issued on 14 May 1281 by King Edward I when he announced that a hunter named Peter Corbett was licensed to capture and destroy wolves in Gloucestershire, Worcestershire, Herefordshire, Shropshire and Staffordshire.

*The Master of Game* is an early fifteenth century hunting treatise, translated from French by Edward III's grandson, the Duke of Aumarle. Although other hunting treatises were circulating in England at that time, this contains the most information about wolves. The author excludes French chapters on the ibex and bear as these animals were not common in England but retained the section on wolves. This may have been for literary purposes but suggests that wolves were still known in England.

The last record of a nobleman being granted land in return for destroying wolves is in 1439. During the reign of Henry VI Robert Umfraville held the castle of Herbotell and manor of Otterburn by virtue of keeping the valley of Riddlesdale free from wolves and robbers. Again wolves were associated with the criminal, existing beyond the boundaries of conventional human societies.

Wolves were mentioned by John Manwood in his treatise of 1567, although he did not believe they were still in England then, but they do not appear in later treatises. In 1576 George Turbevile wrote a book on hunting in which he said that wolves did not exist in England but were common in Ireland and France. Phillip Sidney told German scholars in 1577 that no wolves existed in England outside private collections (Holtgen 1981). He referred to an ancient law which allowed some criminals to avoid punishment by procuring wolf heads and tongues. This is probably connected to a statement by William of Malmesbury that no wolves existed in Wales because King Edgar had demanded a tribute of three hundred wolves each year from the country (William of Malmesbury 1128 (1883: 2.8)). William was wrong as wolves are known to have survived in Wales well into the fifteenth century and perhaps beyond. Yet his statement was seized upon as fact by many later commentators.

## No more wolves in England

The generally accepted view is that wolves became extinct in England at the start of the sixteenth century. There are local stories that the last ones were killed in the New Forest in the late fourteenth century, at Bolton Priory in Wharfedale in 1306, at Wormhill, Derbyshire *circa* 1350, and in Whitby in 1396. Given that wolves survived in Scotland until the seventeenth century they probably remained in the northern regions of England until at least the early sixteenth century. The rolls of

Whitby Abbey show the tanning of thirteen wolf skins in 1395, suggesting that several lived in that area. In the south it was probably a different story. We know that four imported wolf skins reached London in the early fourteenth century and were intended for use in medicine (Thomas 1925: 51). By this time it may have been impossible to find wolves closer to home.

The precise date of the wolf's departure from English soil might never be confirmed. Equally problematic are the reasons for the extinction as other parts of the British Isles and most of mainland Europe sustained a population for much longer. Possibly the increased economic importance of the wool trade led to extensive hunting campaigns but there is no evidence of this. The elimination of wolves in Scotland, Ireland and Wales did not coincide with the expansion of the wool trade in those countries. There are several proverbs on the wolf and sheep theme. These include 'While you trust to the dog the wolf slips into the sheepfold', 'Two wolves may worry one sheep' and 'Dust raised by the sheep doesn't choke the wolf.' The first extant record of these three proverbs in England is in the eighteenth century so it is unlikely that they were used in campaigns against the wolf (Smith 1948). Indeed they are more humorous than hostile.

Although wolves were hunted in England, nothing indicates a sustained, widespread national campaign aimed at eliminating them. Noblemen who received land for their services in destroying wolves would not have benefited from removing them entirely as they needed to demonstrate, if asked, that they were still actively hunting. Factors such as the destruction of woodland habitat, a decline of prey species and disease may have contributed to the decline. Maybe the population of wolves in England was never very high. The virtual absence of wolves in extant mediaeval writings would suggest this.

Large areas of England's woodlands had been cleared for cultivation or grazing by the early fourteenth century. On the continent the process was accelerated in the nineteenth century which coincides with a reduction in the wolf population. Wolves are versatile creatures but large populations cannot survive if deprived of their preferred habitat and the prey that live there.

## Contemporary opinions on the extinction of wolves in England

Question six in the survey asked the respondents to state in which century wolves became extinct in England. The objective was to see how well-informed they were.

The answers of the 172 respondents who answered this question are listed opposite.

The majority of the respondents felt that wolves became extinct between the seventeenth century and the present day. This may be because these centuries are associated with economic progress. The results do indicate a lack of knowledge about the history of wolves in England.

Whatever the reasons wolves vanished from England but beliefs about them remained. The development of newspapers and increased international travel reinforced these beliefs with stories about wolves in other countries.

*'In which century did wolves became extinct in England?'*

| Century | Number of Respondents |
|---|---|
| 5<sup>th</sup> | 2 |
| 7<sup>th</sup> | 1 |
| 10<sup>th</sup> | 1 |
| 11<sup>th</sup> | 3 |
| 12<sup>th</sup> | 6 |
| 13<sup>th</sup> | 5 |
| 14<sup>th</sup> | 4 |
| 15<sup>th</sup> | 10 |
| 16<sup>th</sup> | 13 |
| 17<sup>th</sup> | 24 |
| 18<sup>th</sup> | 43 |
| 19<sup>th</sup> | 33 |
| 20<sup>th</sup> | 10 |
| Not extinct | 7 |
| Don't know | 11 |

**Newspaper reports about wolves**

During the nineteenth century there were sporadic reports of wolf or wolf-like creatures in England. A long report in the 29 April 1834 edition of *The Times* described an escape from the Tower of London menagerie the previous year. Wolves had been kept at the tower for centuries and this was the first recorded escape. The animal harassed the wife of a guard before being recaptured. The report stresses the wolf's brutality and the fear of the lady.

On 16 December 1839 *The Times* reported the presence of four large wolves near Lilleshall, Salop. One was killed and the others captured. This information came from the *Shrewsbury Herald*. Nobody knows where they came from or where they went. Before the passing of the Dangerous Wild Animals Act in 1976 people could keep wolves, and other wild animals, without the authorities being informed.

Currently each local authority is obliged to maintain a register although there is no national database.

In 1843 a Russian wolf escaped from a fair owned by a Mr Wright in Coventry and was recaptured (*The Times* 29 June 1843: 7). In December of that year two wolves also escaped from a fair owned by Mr Wright; it is not clear if he was the same keeper. The second escape was in Ashton. One wolf was killed but the second survived, retaining sufficient strength to bite its keeper (*The Times* 9 December 1843: 6). In 1869 a Siberian wolf escaped from a menagerie near Liverpool (*The Times* 9 February 1869: 5). Again it was recaptured.

In November 1865 *The Times* reported a half-wolf attacking sheep in villages near Harrogate (*The Times* 11 November 1865: 12). This animal was never caught or identified. Modern studies in countries where wolves still exist frequently show wolves being blamed for atrocities proven to have committed by dogs or other canids such as foxes or coyotes. Without evidence it is difficult to say that this was the case in Harrogate but it remains a strong possibility.

In 1884 it was speculated that wolves were living in Epping Forest, after a coyote was found there. Rumour said that a man called Fletcher had brought four cubs to England some years before and abandoned them in the forest (*The Times* 21 July 1884: 10). Subsequent correspondence disputed this with comments about the misidentification of canids but the president of the zoological gardens confirmed that the animal was indeed a prairie wolf (coyote). No more is said of the other cubs alleged to have been released in the forest.

In February 1888 eight wolves escaped, or were freed by bitter grooms, from Sanger's circus in Westminster and attacked some horses (*The Times* 13 February 1888: 6 and 14 February 1888). Although no people were attacked the wolves were considered by the journalist at least to be a danger to the public. An interesting comparison can be made with twentieth century newspaper reports of big cat sightings in the UK. In almost every instance the media suggest that the cats may be a danger to the public although there is no evidence to support this view. These felid predators are often blamed for the destruction of sheep and other animals with similar unexplained incidents in the nineteenth century being attributed to wolves. Anyone interested in big cat sightings in Britain is advised to read *Mystery Big Cats* by Merrily Harpur (Harpur 2006).

During the nineteenth century *The Times* periodically reported the presence of wolves in France, making stories out of attacks on sheep and horses as well as more sensational accounts featuring human victims. There is a patronising tone about some of the accounts, reminding readers that wild beasts no longer existed in England. The reports describing wolf attacks on humans are examined in more detail in Chapter Two.

While most Victorians read reports about escaped wolves in England and ferocious ones eating humans on the continent, with some trepidation a Bolton publican named William Entwhistle decided, for reasons unknown, to walk around a cage

*Early twentieth century postcard from a photograph of the Allendale wolf.*

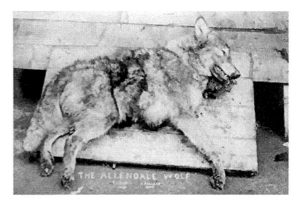

containing a pack of Siberian wolves with a female companion in 1891. His bravery was commented upon by *The Times* reporter (*The Times* 9 January 1891: 7).

## A wolf in Northumberland

In December 1904 a wolf was reported in Hexham, Northumberland. For a period of about three weeks farmers reported loss of livestock and blamed it on a wolf. A local man, Captain Bain of Shotley Bridge, had lost his pet wolf three months earlier and informed the local constabulary. Several hunts were organised and various sightings occurred. The area was in a state of panic, due to the belief that the wolf presented a danger to children, until the 30th December when a wolf was killed by a train near Cumwhinton, four miles from Carlisle and 30 miles from the area plagued by the wolf. Despite Captain Bain's insistence that this was not his wolf and some later sightings, it seems likely that this was the animal responsible. A photograph taken by a railway porter still survives, it is even featured on local postcards, and the resemblance to a wolf is striking. A local beer is called the Allendale Wolf after this creature.

## Later sightings of the wolf in England

There have been recent sightings of wolves in England and other parts of the British Isles. In August 2003 one was reported on Saddleworth Way in the Pennines, and a lady called Irene Carruthers saw two grey wolves in her garden in the village of Eaglesfield between Gretna and Lockerbie in October 2003 (Meredith 2003). In Dorset a pensioner saw a wolf in August 2003 (Fraser 2003). No explanation, other than mistaken identity, has been put forward to account for these sightings.

## The wolf in classical texts

For the last six hundred years at least most English people have not been in a position to judge wolves by direct observation. Their impressions of the animal depended on what they were told or, for the educated, read. There are several important surviving natural history texts from the ancient world, which describe wolves and were known in England. Like current zoologists the authors of these works wished to record the results of observations, although rarely their own. They seemed content to commit all their zoological knowledge, including legend and hyperbole to paper. Most relied on second-hand information which they had no means of verifying.

Aristotle wrote three such treatises, *On the Generation of Animals, Parts of Animals*, and *Historia Animalium*. It is in the latter, *circa* 344–342 BC, that he makes specific comments about wolves. He describes them, like the leopard, as always wild, true to its own type and scheming. Aristotle was concerned with the classification of animals and sought to establish connections between different species. He recognised the uniqueness of wolves in one respect, namely that they were the only animal to eat earth. This is incorrect. Wolves will digest soil but so do other animals.

Aristotle stated that adversaries of wolves included pigs, asses, bulls and foxes. All four are creatures which wolves will eat. One negative story, which he relates, tells how wolves near the sea of Azoz destroyed the nets of fishermen who refused to share their catch. This is not described as a hostile action however and Aristotle reserves judgement. His is reserved and compact, offering an accurate record of natural history in many respects. Unfortunately the *Historia Animalium* was less influential in England than the works of Pliny and Aelian which followed it but drifted more frequently from records of scientific observation into speculation and legend.

## Natural history?

Pliny the Elder completed his mammoth work, *Natural History*, around AD 77. He is rare among ancient writers in acknowledging sources although he does not directly attribute information to specific authors. He took Aristotle's point about wolves feeding on earth and described it as an augury. If a wolf did this in large mouthfuls when barring the path of travellers on the right-hand side it was the finest of omens. He stated that no wolves existed on Mount Olympus or in Crete. According to him the wolf, like the hyena and lion, had a stiff nape. This may be related to the story that when a man and woman met, whoever spied the other first would strike him dumb and this injury made it impossible for the wolf to turn away. This 'striking dumb' belief persisted in literature until the seventeenth century and also appeared in bestiaries and the manuals of witch-hunters.

Pliny's achievements in collating such a mass of material are undermined by his credibility. He speaks of enormous snakes swallowing stags and the sky raining iron, blood, milk and wool. However he is not hostile to wolves in any way nor does he refer to them as eaters of humans.

## Aelian on wolves

Chronologically the next important text was *On the Characteristics of Animals* by Claudius Aelianus in the early third century AD. He believed in advancing the good qualities of animals to illustrate the failings of individual humans. His text is a blend of Pliny's research with the Aesopic fable, which occupied an important place in the mediaeval curriculum. He described Crete as hostile to wolves and reptiles and learnt from Theophrastus, rather than Pliny, that there were places on Macedonian Olympus where wolves did not go. No reason is given. He elaborated on Aristotle's comment that the wolf fights with the bull, describing how a wolf attempts to avoid the bull's horns and the feigning of an attack. Cunning is a characteristic often attributed to the wolf by later writers but is more commonly associated with the fox.

Not content with Aristotle's description of the fox as an adversary of the wolf Aelian went on to say that the two animals are at war. He informed us that the wolf goes numb when near the leaves of squill (*Urginea scilla*) and that the fox throws those leaves into wolf dens. In some folktales the role of the fox and wolf are interchangeable. The mediaeval story of Reynard the Fox made Ysengrimus, the wolf, a bitter enemy of the eponymous fox. Some other stories have the fox and wolf working together against the hero animal.

Aelian went on to state that the strength of their claws and sharpness of their fangs makes wolves, leopards and lions bold. In later texts all these predators would be grouped together under the simple classification of 'beasts'. Aelian claims that the neck of the wolf is short and compressed, making the animal look straight ahead and forcing it to turn its whole body. These points are extensions of what Pliny and Aristotle wrote.

Aelian expanded on earlier descriptions of the satiated wolf saying that it became gentle and refrained from attacking humans and beasts. Here he is implying that wolves were known to attack people.

Many later descriptions of wolves can be traced back to Aelian. One has to doubt his veracity however. He tells how wolves swam across rivers by linking their tails in their mouths and then repeats the same story about mice and rats. This repetition, even before one considers the likelihood of the story, ensures that he cannot be considered a reliable commentator on natural history. For a long time his text was used to provide information on wolves simply because there was nothing else available.

**Classification of wolves**

Carl Linnaeus's *System Naturae* was the first attempt since Pliny to classify all animal species. The first edition appeared in 1735. The section on wolves, from an English translation in 1820, reads as follows:

> 'Lupus. Tail bent inwards. Inhabits Europe, Asia, Africa and North America. Hunts in packs and destroys cattle. Suspicious, being hardly heard in the woods, fearful of a rope drawn across the ground, will not pass through a door but leaps over the fence, dreads the sound of a trumpet, exquisite in the art of smelling, patient of extreme hunger and cold, devours man and even his own species, howls in the night and is destroyed by the lichen vulpinum. Female gravid 10 weeks, brings forth 5–9 young which are blind at birth.'

> (Turton 1820 1.15)

*Grey Wolf lying in grass.*

There is then a brief physical description of the animal, identifying four different-coloured species. These were described as yellow in France and Germany, white in Russia, black in Canada and grey tinged with black on the Cape of Good Hope, South Africa. Several subspecies of wolves exist but a yellow one has never been identified and the species common to Canada, Russia and Western Europe is the same.

The ideas that wolves avoid ropes and doors and dread the sound of a trumpet are not found elsewhere. Most animals react to loud sounds and will be cautious with unfamiliar items. Linnaeus's work in places does not appear objective. This was noted in the mid-eighteenth century by an Englishman, John Hill, who wrote his own natural history claiming that, unlike Linnaeus, his research was based on observation. While it is unlikely that Hill personally saw all the animals which he wrote about, his account of wolves is more factual with the possible exception of a remark that wolves attack houses and kill people in hard winters. This belief appears frequently in literature but is not supported by the historical evidence.

## Books about the wolf in England

In 1890 James Harting wrote a history of the wolf in Britain as part of a longer work on extinct mammals. He did not have much to say about wolves attacking people, except to repeat a few legends. He was also unconcerned with wolf behaviour, concentrating on historical and archaeological evidence. By collating this data, often from obscure sources, he provided a valuable service to latter researchers. He did not criticise his sources, showing a respect for them that is typical of his generation.

At the end of his work he states that he neglected superstitious elements, principally meaning werewolves, in order to keep the study short. Others might be tempted to classify the oral legends which he cites in abundance, and with reverence, under the heading 'superstition'.

Harting's work was summarised by Ebenezer Brewer in his dictionary of phrase and fable, which was first published in 1870. Brewer begins by noting that in music 'wolf' denotes a false note on almost all stringed instruments. Then he refers to various proverbs about wolves, citing the origins where known. This is a useful account of beliefs about wolves at the end of the Victorian era and shows how little was known. Zoology was still a young discipline and focused primarily on the capture of animals for Western collections rather than the study of them in their natural habitats.

## Books about wolves in the twentieth century

Scientific texts about wolves were not widely disseminated in England. Books that blended fact and fiction into more accessible prose, like John Pollard's *Wolves and Werewolves*, were more likely to be read by the general public (Pollard 1964). This text is not annotated and contains many myths described as true occurrences. Pollard provides a list of sources although the details are vague. He relied heavily on reports in *The Times*, and in many cases appears to have copied directly from Harting.

Pollard refers to a battle between wolves and humans, implying that both sides contributed to the fight. Chapter headings such as 'The Wolf that Ate the Postman' and 'Killer Wolves in Scotland' indicate the extent to which he was influenced by a belief in bellicose wolves. The postman, along with many of the other alleged victims, is not named.

One of the most popular texts about wolves, often believed to be a factual account, is *Never Cry Wolf* by Farley Mowat. It supposedly contains the results of the author's own observations, conveyed in the first person. The narrator is sent to examine wolves in the Arctic and to assess their impact on the caribou population. During this research he becomes increasingly sceptical about public and official views concerning wolves. In his introduction Mowat states correctly that many of his conclusions have been confirmed by zoologists but not his thesis that the wolf poses no threat to man and is not a competitor of any significance to humans. Twenty-five years later more people are agreeing with him on all points.

*Never Cry Wolf* is important as the first literary text to present an entirely favourable image of the wolf and to portray wolf-hating humans as bigoted and misguided. In the 1970s criticism of governments and official bodies was increasing, and being accepted in Western societies. Public awareness of issues such as environmentalism and conservation was also increasing and attracting voices of dissent. Gradually the wolf became the symbol of a wilderness which people wished to protect. Mowat perhaps did more to challenge negative images of the wolf than the many scientists whose books on the topics stick to factual observations.

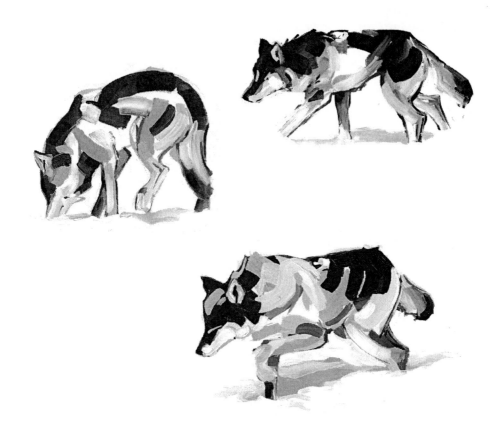

*Paintings of wolves by Esther Tyson, reproduced by kind permission of the artist. Esther and the author participated in an eco-wolf holiday organised by the Wolf Society of Great Britain and the Slovak Wildlife Society in 2003.*

## Changing attitudes

Conveying scientific information to the general public was made easier with the introduction of televised wildlife documentaries. These enabled people to see wolves in the wild for the first time. Early wolf documentaries shown in England concentrated on wolves in Canada or the Arctic. More recently they have shown wolves in Eastern European countries such as Slovakia and Poland. Generally they support the conclusions of Mech, Murie and Linnell and portray wolves as non-dangerous to people. However they do not address the belief in wolves attacking people and the reasons for the existence of this belief.

Other large predators have also featured in television documentaries, leading to increased conservation efforts as more and more people are willing to spend money to see these creatures in the wild. There is a Wolf Society of Great Britain, recently renamed the Wolves and Humans Foundation, which raises funds to promote wolf conservation in other parts of the world. A wolf sanctuary run by the UK Wolf Conservation Trust exists in Reading and wolf eco-holidays in Eastern Europe, Germany, America and Canada are organised by both charities and commercial companies. Often some of the profit is invested in conservation programmes.

There has been a change in public attitude towards wolves that would have been unthinkable a century earlier. The media too has changed emphasis. Reports about wolves in British newspapers today usually take a balanced view of hunting campaigns overseas or discuss the idea of wolf reintroduction in the Highlands without a negative stance. Such views would have been inconceivable a hundred years before when the wolf was portrayed in the media as dangerous to humans and, in many instances, as capable of eating people.

The old image has not disappeared entirely. On 16 December 2005 the BBC broadcast a drama documentary entitled *The Man-Eating Wolves of Gysinge* about an historical incident of wolves attacking humans in Sweden. Evidence uncovered by historians, zoologists and researchers has ascertained the rarity of such incidents. The next chapter will examine some of them in detail.

# Chapter two

# Wolf attacks on people

Several animal species including lions, leopards, snakes and gorillas have been accused of eating humans. Some of these do attack and eat people. However reported deaths during the twentieth century show that the fear of 'man-eating' animals is disproportionate to the number of verified instances. Animals killing people in order to eat them seems to be a rare occurrence. It is not a normal pattern of behaviour for any species.

**The lone wolf**

Attacks on humans by large cats tend to be by old individuals unable to hunt their normal prey. They probably became accustomed to human flesh by chance as a result of scavenging on corpses. This was believed to be the case with the famous man-eating leopard of Rudraprayag in India, killed by the British hunter Jim Corbett in 1926. The pattern has also been observed in tigers.

For humans who seek control over the natural world it is unsettling to acknowledge that predators find it easier to kill them than other animals. Consequently people would rather believe that they are threatened by a powerful pack than by an individual animal which has been ejected, through age, inability or injury from that pack.

In fiction packs of wolves are often presented as more dangerous to humans than a single wolf. Several ancient and mediaeval commentators stated that single wolves rather than packs were eating people. Aristotle said that man-eating was a trait of single wolves and Pausanias claimed that the wolf was more savage than wolves (Aristotle 1991: 7.5; Pausanias 1979 Vol. 1: 297). The Duke of Aumarle said that old and weak wolves attacked humans. (Edward 1909: 60).

Wolves are a social species who usually hunt in packs. Lone wolves fall into three categories in respect of their relationship to the rest of the pack: trailing subordinates, socially unacceptable scavengers, and independent animals. These can be classified as followers, those unwanted elsewhere and those who chose temporarily to be alone. A study in Alaska found a 26 percent dispersal rate from the pack, mostly males who entered other packs (Jordan 1967: 243). Some who leave will return. Temporary splitting is common and generally it is subordinate wolves and young adults who depart from the pack. Albert the Great made what he described as a personal observation that injured wolves leave the pack (Albert the Great 1989: 22.68). Barry Lopez thought it possible that wolves with contagious diseases would be expelled from the pack (Lopez 1978: 52). According to Erik Zimen hunger leads to aggression and a weakening of social bonds, both of which favour emigration from the pack (Zimen 1980: 242). The lone wolf metaphor was first coined in twentieth-century America and has been used to describe mavericks and people who take risks. This recognises, and often admires, humans who avoid social contact with their peers.

By not hunting with other wolves the lone wolf fails to conform to normal wolf standards of behaviour. Hunting techniques normally adopted by wolves require the co-operation of the pack. The lone wolf cannot catch large ungulates and must exist by scavenging on smaller mammals. It is capable of catching a small child.

The vast majority of attacks by non-rabid wolves on humans recorded by Linnell's team involved single wolves. This pattern seems even more likely in areas where the wolf is in close contact with unescorted children, as was the case in mediaeval Europe and is now the case in India and other parts of the world. Because of their size children would be easy targets for a hungry wolf.

### Contemporary opinions on packs of wolves attacking people

Question ten of the survey asked those respondents who felt that wolves were dangerous to people to state if they considered a pack of wolves or a lone wolf to be more dangerous. Of the 137 respondents who replied to this question, 100 felt that a pack of wolves were more dangerous than a single wolf. This contradicts the historical evidence, implying that the respondents were more influenced by other sources such as fiction and that their knowledge of wolves is limited.

### Wolf attacks on people in Britain

In the British Isles there are some extant stories of wolves killing humans, mostly recorded in obscure legends and local traditions. Their influence in previous times is hard to assess but they would have been spread by word-of-mouth in the immediate locality at least.

The Scottish chronicler Andrew of Wyntoun tells how an early British king, Memprys, was killed by a wolf while out hunting (Andrew 1903 Vol.1:54). The king was supposed to be a direct descendant of Brutus who died in 980 BC but the story was not written down until 1480 so cannot be considered reliable. Memprys is mentioned by Richard Rowlands, known as Verstegan, who claims that another early British king, Mada, was also slain by wolves (Verstegan 1605: 59)

Two legends hail from Cumberland. Near Ulpha in Millom parish there is a well called Lady's Dub. Tradition said that a lady was killed by wolves in the vicinity (Whelan 1860: 411). Another lady, the wife of the Lord of Beckerment, was also supposedly killed by wolves while hunting (Whelan 1860: 463). Neither story can be dated.

In England the virtual absence of references to wolf attacks in extant sources does not mean that wolves did not eat people. There are stories that wolves were thought by the Anglo-Saxons to be more dangerous in winter. There is no contemporary evidence to support this but the writers who recorded the belief may have had access to sources which no longer survive. Olaus Magnus, who wrote in 1555 with an English translation in 1658, implied that wolves were more dangerous to people in January (Magnus 1658: 18.10). Delabere Blaine quoted an unnamed ancient authority who said that the Saxons called January 'wolf-month' because they were more likely to be devoured at that time (Blaine 1800 (1852: 104)). This comment also appears in Verstegan's wonderfully titled *Restitution of Decayed Intelligence* (Verstegan 1605: 69). The correct Saxon name for January was *Æftera-geol-monab* meaning 'after Yuletide month'.

Wolves have more difficulty hunting their normal prey in severe winters and travel more in search of food. This may have led to increased predation on domestic animals and therefore more interaction with humans. Yet evidence that the Anglo-Saxons believed in man-eating wolves is sparse. The evidence of names, mentioned in the last chapter, suggests that they respected rather than feared wolves.

Olaus Magnus said that some of the northern people would receive arms at church in order to defend themselves against wolves (Magnus 1658: 18.10). According to him those wolves preferred big-bellied women. He also said that small wolves were found in Africa and Egypt but the northern wolves were fiercer. In expressing these sentiments he was copying earlier writers. Herodotus stated that Egyptian wolves were the size of foxes and Pliny commented that African and Egyptian wolves were feebler than their cruel and fierce counterparts elsewhere (Herodotus 1996: 2.67; Pliny 1960: 8.80). This indicates that ancient writers were not always adept at distinguishing wolves from other canids.

## Wolves eating corpses

Some Anglo-Saxon and early Norman poems imply that wolves ate corpses on battlefields and others associate wolves with death and battle. The Anglo-Norman poet Guido describes wolves feeding on the dead in the aftermath of the Battle of Hastings and animals that resemble wolves are depicted on the Bayeux tapestry with long tongues licking their front paws. There is nothing implausible about the carrion-eating wolf consuming bodies which had been abandoned on the battlefield or in other locations, such as those close to the gallows. Many bodies would not be buried deeply and during times of plague would be exposed in numbers.

If wolves were seen eating corpses then it is not hard to see why stories about them eating living people were accepted. The hyena, often confused with the wolf, is a scavenger that does feed on corpses. Some mediaeval bestiaries contain illustrations showing the hyena taking bodies from tombs.

Timotheus of Gaza informs us that the hyena mated with the wolf to produce a lone wolf that preyed on humans and animals (Bodenheimer and Rabinowitz 1950: 4.4). This beast may have been the Crocutta which was mentioned by several ancient

*'Hunters: Have You Seen.'*
*A poster distributed by the*
*US Fish and Wildlife Service*
*to advise hunters on how to*
*identify grey wolves.*
*Reproduced by kind*
*permission of the US Fish*
*and WildlifeService.*

**HUNTERS: HAVE YOU SEEN?**

Recognizing A Gray Wolf

- 2.5 feet tall
- 5-6 feet long
- 80-100 pounds
- Broad snout
- Round ears
- Color varies from black to white
- Long, low howl

ACTUAL SIZE

Wolves are protected by federal law under the Endangered Species Act.

The U.S . Forest Service and U.S. Fish & Wildlife Service request that hunters report any sightings or wolf sign. Please make these reports to the MT FishWildlife & Parks, local Forest Service office, or the U.S. Fish & Wildlife Service at (406) 449-5225.

Information provided by hunters will aid in the management and eventual removal of wolves from the endangered species list.
Thank you for your cooperation.

writers. It was allegedly capable of imitating human speech and could lure humans to their deaths by calling out their names in the same way that mermaids were thought to bewitch sailors. Linnaeus included the Crocutta in his *System Naturae*, defining it as the spotted hyena which dwelt in Guinea, Ethiopia and the Cape of Good Hope in South Africa (Turton 1820: 44). He considered it to be an eater of people. Were wolves typecast as man-eaters because of the perceived behaviour of similar canid species?

### Confusion between canid species

In 1972 George Kolenosky described an experiment in which a captive female wolf was bred with a male coyote (Kolenosky 1972). Two litters, instead of the usual one, were produced. This demonstrated that hybridization occurred between wolves and coyotes. Wolves also interbreed with dogs. The animals produced by these liaisons are often dangerous to people. One hybrid described as 97 percent like a timber wolf attacked a human in July 1997 (*Memphis Commercial Appeal* 10 July 1997). A year earlier another American woman was killed by two hybrid canids in front of her children (*Lexington Herald Leader* 18 December 1996). In previous times distinctions would not be readily made between wolves, canids that resembled wolves, and hybrids.

This confusion continued into the twentieth century. Anthony Dent felt that Alsatian dogs left by retreating German soldiers at the end of World War II contributed to reports of wolves in France at that time (Dent 1979:13). Erik Zimen described how it proved impossible to convince some Italian villagers that a dead animal in front of them was a dog and not a wolf (Zimen 1980: 298). Barry Lopez referred to a North Dakota rancher who blamed wolves for damage that was committed by his own dog. (Lopez 1978: 197). Misidentification between wolves and coyotes remains common.

There are instances of non-diseased coyotes attacking children in North America. In a study of these attacks Lu Carbyn concluded that the individual animals were those which had lost their fear of people (Carbyn 1989: 444–6). Adult coyotes with young were more persistent in their attacks. Despite this the coyote is not generally regarded as dangerous, demonstrating that individual perceptions of the natural world are based on ideas rather than facts. Since only a few trained experts can distinguish between wolves, wolf-hybrids and other canids resembling wolves it is possible that wolves were and are blamed for the actions of these other animals.

Wolves are symbolic of the wild and the untamed. They are also considered to be larger than other canids and have an evil reputation. Humans find it easier to imagine wolves attacking them than coyotes or domestic dogs doing the same. Other canid species live closer to humans and admitting the danger they sometimes pose could cause panic.

### Reasons why wolves might eat humans

Some mediaeval texts began to postulate reasons why individual wolves ate humans. *The Master of Game* describes wolves as strong and evil, noting that they fed on flesh, carrion and vermin. The author felt that a wolf which had eaten a person would become addicted to the taste and would then pursue other humans. Apparently it had been known for wolves to leave sheep untouched and eat the shepherd instead (Edward 1909: 60–1). This would be very abnormal behaviour for a wolf.

In 1508 a German preacher, Geiler Von Kaysersberg, published a sermon which listed seven reasons why wolves eat humans. Although this may not have been disseminated in England during the sixteenth century many of the reasons have appeared in sources that were, such as *The Master of Game*. The reasons given are hunger, savageness, age, experience, madness, the Devil and God.

The text of this extraordinary sermon, as translated by Sabine Baring Gould, is as follows:

> What shall we say about were-wolves? for there are were-wolves which run about the villages devouring men and children. As men say about them, they run about full gallop, injuring men, and are called *ber-wölff*, or *wer-wölff*. Do you ask me if I know aught about them? I answer, Yes. They are apparently wolves which eat men and children, and that happens on seven accounts:
>
> 1. *Esuriem* – Hunger.
> 2. *Rabiem* – Savageness.
> 3. *Senectutem* – Old age.

4. *Experientiam* – Experience.
5. *Insaniem* – Madness.
6. *Diabolum* – The Devil.
7. *Deum* – God.

The first happens through hunger; when the wolves find nothing to eat in the woods; they must come to people and eat men when hunger drives them to it. You see well, when it is very cold, that the stags come in search of food up to the villages, and the birds actually into the dining-room in search of victuals.

Under the second head, wolves eat children through their innate savageness, because they are savage, and that is (*propter locum coitum ferum*). Their savageness arises first from their condition. Wolves which live in cold places are smaller on that account, and more savage than other wolves. Secondly, their savageness depends on the season; they are more savage about Candlemas than at any other time of the year, and men must be more on their guard against them then than at other times. It is a proverb, 'He who seeks a wolf at Candlemas, a peasant on Shrove Tuesday, and a parson in Lent, is a man of pluck.' [...] Thirdly, their savageness depends on their having young. When the wolves have young, they are more savage than when they have not. You see it so in all beasts. A wild duck, when it has young poults, you see what an uproar it makes. A cat fights for its young kittens; the wolves do ditto.

Under the third head, the wolves do injury on account of their age. When a wolf is old, it is weak and feeble in its legs, so it can't ran fast enough to catch stags, and therefore it rends a man, whom it can catch easier than a wild animal. It also tears children and men easier than wild animals, because of its teeth, for its teeth break off when it is very old; you see it well in old women: how the last teeth wobble, and they have scarcely a tooth left in their heads, and they open their mouths for men to feed them with mash and stewed substances.

Under the fourth head, the injury the were-wolves do arises from experience. It is said that human flesh is far sweeter than other flesh; so when a wolf has once tasted human flesh, he desires to taste it again. So he acts like old topers, who, when they know the best wine, will not be put off with inferior quality.

Under the fifth head, the injury arises from ignorance. A dog when it is mad is also inconsiderate, and it bites any man; it does not recognize its own lord: and what is a wolf but a wild dog which is mad and inconsiderate, so that it regards no man.

Under the sixth head, the injury comes of the Devil, who transforms himself, and takes on him the form of a wolf so writes

Vincentius in his *Speculum Historiale*. And he has taken it from Valerius Maximus in the Punic war. When the Romans fought against the men of Africa, when the captain lay asleep, there came a wolf and drew his sword, and carried it off. That was the Devil in a wolf's form. The like writes William of Paris, that a wolf will kill and devour children, and do the greatest mischief. There was a man who had the phantasy that he himself was a wolf. And afterwards he was found lying in the wood, and he was dead out of sheer hunger.

Under the seventh head, the injury comes of God's ordinance. For God will sometimes punish certain lands and villages with wolves. So we read of Elisha, that when Elisha wanted to go up a mountain out of Jericho, some naughty boys made a mock of him and said, 'O bald head, step up! O glossy pate, step up!' What happened? He cursed them. Then came two bears out of the desert and tore about forty-two of the children. That was God's ordinance. The like we read of a prophet who would set at naught the commands he had received of God, for he was persuaded to eat bread at the house of another. As he went home he rode upon his ass. Then came a lion which slew him and left the ass alone. That was God's ordinance. Therefore must man turn to God when He brings wild beasts to do him a mischief: which same brutes may He not bring now or evermore. Amen.

(Baring-Gould 1865)

Three of the reasons given by the preacher – hunger, age and injury – are closely related. The pattern of elderly and injured animal predators attacking people is commonly found. Variations do exist in the hunting behaviour of wolves. They adapt according to their environment and can develop individual hunting techniques.

The first five reasons put forward by the preacher are scientific rather than supernatural. He has sought logical explanations for wolves eating people but attacks on humans by wolves must have been rare to merit this search. If it was widely accepted that wolves preyed on people then Von Kaysersberg would not have needed to postulate reasons why individual wolves did so. However he does not refer to specific instances and his point about savageness being innate in wolves is contradictory as he acknowledges that not all wolves eat humans.

## Wolf attacks on people in France

Although wolves became extinct in England earlier than on the continent, a belief in wolves attacking people was reinforced by reports from overseas. A diary of Parisian life at the start of the fifteenth century makes a few references to man-eating wolves. The author tells us that wolves came into towns, swimming across rivers and digging up corpses. (Anon. 1450 (1958: 162)). In March 1420 wolves which had entered the city to eat corpses were attracted to a pregnant woman who had been tied to a tree

*Contemporary drawing of the Beast of Gevaudan.*

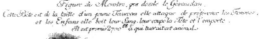

and they then devoured her (Anon. 1450 (1958: 175)). In a more specific case a child was eaten by a wolf in the Place aux Chats in 1438 (Anon. 1450 (1958: 327)). In another incident during the last week of September 1439, wolves apparently killed and ate fourteen people (Anon. 1450, (1958: 332)). They ignored herds and attacked herdsmen. One wolf called Courtaud, a name usually given to a docked horse, was caught on Martinmas Eve (10th November).

The story of Courtaud was exaggerated into an epic tale by later writers, some of whom wrote for an English-speaking audience. In his mixture of fiction and legend Ernest Seton tells of the hunter Boisselier and the wolf-king of France, Courtaud (Seton 1937: 261–90). After a long and vicious battle, hunter and prey perished together. The anonymous contemporary diarist does not mention this. He does state that on 16 December 1439, a wolf killed four housewives. The next day sixteen more people were wounded and eleven died (Anon. 1450 (1958: 332)). This high casualty rate may have resulted from attacks by a rabid wolf, as a sane animal would not have reason to attack so many people. Certainly it would not have been able to eat them all. No precise details are given for any of the victims and it is unclear if the writer witnessed the events. However, his precise dates indicate a degree of reliability, and someone writing a private document had no reason to invent the stories.

## La Bete du Gevaudan

The most famous man-eating wolf is the beast of the Gevaudan, a region in southern France. This animal was considered to be responsible for the deaths of up to 113 people between 1764 and 1767. The story was first reported to the international media through *The Gazette de France* in April 1765, nine months after the ravages began. Crucial eyewitness accounts, if written down at all, are now distorted and difficult to accept as historical evidence. Richard Thompson has written a full-length book in English which tells the story.

The deaths were reported between July 1764 and June 1767 when they ceased, following the shooting of a wolf. In September 1765 another oversize wolf had been killed and, erroneously, proclaimed as the beast. Thompson believed that the animal responsible for the deaths was a wolf, albeit one acting abnormally. This was not always the view of contemporaries who attributed the animal with supernatural powers and could not agree on its identity.

Contemporary views now only survive in newspaper reports and later texts. According to these sources the beast was described alternately as a wolf, a werewolf, a lynx, a bear, a punishment sent by God and an unknown animal. Precise identification is not now possible and, as previously discussed, there is ample evidence from modern times that wolves are confused with other canid species and serious errors made. Since the people in the Gevaudan were gripped by hysteria, resulting from the beast's antics, possible distortions would easily arise.

Statistics from the Gevaudan relating to fatalities and attack patterns are important when compared with the observed behaviour of wolves today. There are several anomalies in the pattern of the attacks. Sometimes there would be months without any followed by several in the space of a few days. Generally wolves only eat when hungry. They do not consume one meal then immediately seek another, especially if they have to travel to obtain it. The figures from the Gevaudan contain a number of gaps between recorded attacks. Any animal feeding so irregularly could not survive unless it supplemented its diet with domestic animals, rodents, rabbits and other small mammals. Wolves tend to have one preferred prey species so a wolf which preyed on people would have a consistent attack pattern.

There are reports that the beast of Gevaudan was seen in villages, some miles apart, on the same day. This and the eventual killing of two supposed beasts suggest that there could have been more than one animal involved. Given the rarity of wolves eating people the presence of two in the same area at the same time is unlikely unless human predation is hereditary or caused by environmental conditions. As far as can be ascertained, conditions in the Gevaudan were comparable with those earlier in the eighteenth century and with similar areas around Europe, yet there are no other reliable reports of wolves attacking humans on this scale.

One possibility is that wolf-dog hybrids were responsible. A liaison between a wolf and a sheepdog could have produced the beast. If this was the case then it has to be asked why similar beasts are not about today.

The beast's behaviour did not conform to any of the abnormalities that may induce human predation in wolves. It was demonstrably agile and fit and therefore not resorting to human flesh because of an inability to catch other prey. A wolf preying on people would be expected to target single victims as the easiest to catch. However, many of the victims were shepherds or cowherds slain in front of their flocks or herds. No sane wolf will risk attacking an adult human, which it cannot guarantee to kill, when it could easily steal an animal. Nor will it attack groups of people. As the beast was cunning enough to hide from searchers it clearly did not suffer from insanity, and a rabid animal can be ruled out due to the length of time that it was active. Ultimately the absence of a body prevents an accurate identification of the beast. The second corpse was sent to Versailles but has not been preserved there.

### English reports on the beast

Horace Walpole viewed the body of the beast in Versailles in October 1765 and referred to it in three letters. In the first he stated that it was definitely a wolf and left behind a 'dowager and four young princes.' (Walpole 1820 Vol. 3: 75) In a second letter, on the same day, he notes the extraordinary size of the beast (Walpole 1820 Vol.3: 79). Three days later he commented that it was extremely large and that some people associated it with the Devil (Walpole 1820 Vol.3: 80).

Historical records suggest that there have been 683 deaths caused by non-rabid wolves in France (Linnell 2002: 20). None of the other cases were on the same scale as the beast of Gevaudan or known in England to the same extent. Peter Beckford wrote a hunting treatise in 1798 in which he stated that 20,000 Frenchmen had failed to kill the beast (Beckford 1798: 318). Eighty years later Robert Louis Stevenson travelled through the Gevaudan and named the beast as Napoleon (Stevenson 1879 (1965: 41)) He claimed that it had been active for ten months, chased armed horsemen and turned out to be an ordinary, small wolf which had killed one hundred children. The exaggeration had started.

In 2002 Nick Blackstock wrote a novel entitled *Beast* which was based on the Gevaudan incident. The previous year a French film called *Brotherhood of the Wolf,* loosely based on the beast of Gevaudan, opened in English cinemas. It portrayed the beast as a deformed lion brought back from Africa and controlled by a group of priests who were using the concept of divine punishment to threaten the king. This film which is the most successful, in financial terms, of all French films should not be confused with the fantasy book of the same title, written by David Farland. The real beast of Gevaudan may never be identified, but suggestions, based on hyperbole, will continue to come along.

### Victorian newspaper reports

In the nineteenth century stories of wolves eating people were circulating in English newspapers. *The Times* reports a number of incidents in which humans were attacked and sometimes eaten by wolves in various European countries, Canada, the USA and India. Statistics cited in the newspaper refer to considerably more victims, conveying the impression that wolves were habitual predators on humans.

If the reports and statistics in *The Times* are accurate then two reasons might account for the increase in the number of wolves attacking people. Firstly, the ability to report these instances were previously inferior so local news might not always be relayed to Britain. By the late nineteenth century communication between England and the continent was quicker and newspapers had expanded with more space to report a wider variety of stories. *The Times* reported French news on a daily basis and the newspaper could be purchased in certain parts of France.

The second possible explanation is that the preferred forest habitats of the wolf were being eroded by rapid industrialisation. The resulting reduction in the numbers of prey species would have led to greater interaction between wolves and humans. The wolves became more visible and could no longer hide in the dwindling forests. They would be increasingly likely to prey on domestic animals, and a number of reports refer to casual encounters between humans and wolves. Wolves today tend to distance themselves from people wherever possible but rapid environmental changes in the nineteenth century made this difficult. However the accuracy of the reports in *The Times* must be challenged.

Linnell's team excluded newspaper reports which were not confirmed by other sources, although some cases reported simultaneously by two different newspapers were included. Decisions on reliability were made on each individual case. The following incidents were verified by Linnell's team for the nineteenth century.

+ 380 cases of wolf attacks on humans in France between 1800 and 1900.

+ 112 cases of wolf attacks on humans in the Padania region (modern Italy and Switzerland) between 1800 and 1821.

+ 31 humans killed by wolves in Latvia during the nineteenth century.

+ 31 humans attacked by a wolf in Sweden between 1820 and 1821.

+ Several wolf attacks on people in Finland during the nineteenth century.

+ A girl killed by a wolf in Norway in 1880.

+ Several children carried off by wolves in the Dumoh district of Madhya Pradesh, India in 1890.

+ Three cases of wolves attacking humans in America during the nineteenth century.

+ 273 attacks by wolves on humans in Russia between 1840 and 1861.

Any incidents reported in *The Times*, or elsewhere, but not noted by Linnell must be treated with caution. Earlier writers accepted them as fact and often repeated them without checking the information. It is easy to understand why. Very little was written about wolves in the nineteenth century and newspapers are both preserved and readily accessible. Finding articles in *The Times* was made easier by Palmer's index which for the period 1790–1905 classifies 96 reports with the term 'wolves' and 286 under 'wolf.' Not all are about wolves. They include the usage of phrases such as 'wolves in sheep's clothing', descriptions of individuals as wolves, and people with the surname or first name Wolf who were indicted for criminal offences or made bankrupt. A large number of people had this name in the nineteenth century, most of whom were Polish or Russian Jewish immigrants. There were 134 reports featuring real wolves; the principal ones relating to man-eating wolves are summarised below with some comments.

## Reports on man-eating wolves in *The Times*

25 January 1785
Hunters in Orciers and neighbouring districts had killed ten wolves that were responsible for the deaths of several men and women and a greater number of children.

3 July 1801
On 6 June 1801 a large wolf was killed at Nievre in France. This had supposedly devoured seventeen people and was described as being 'five feet long and thirty two inches high, resembled a greyhound to the body, the head and the neck were white, its muzzle long and jointed and its shoulders covered with thicker and longer hair than that of ordinary wolves.' Linnell's research indicates that seventeen children were killed by a wolf or wolves in Varzy in 1801 (Linnell 2002: 57). Varzy is in the Nievre region so this would appear to be the same incident.

11 February 1825
A French physician, M. Taphanel, discovered a large wolf eating a man. Despite being badly bitten he succeeded in shooting the wolf. The body of the other man was too badly disfigured to be identified.

1 October 1825
This cites a report from the *Journal de Frankfurt* which said that there were large numbers of wolves in the Polish districts of Lubin and Zamoksi. They had killed one child and wounded several people. Here we have an English newspaper citing a German newspaper's account of events in Poland. The information is third hand, at best.

13 October 1825
This cites reports from some unnamed Paris papers. A wolf had terrorised various places in the city. Fifteen people had been wounded with four fatalities. The wolf when dead was described as a female of the 'ordinary species'. This is interesting as it makes a distinction between different species of wolves and also because an individual animal from what was considered the 'normal species' was attacking people.

15 September 1826
On 14 August 1826 a girl named Barbara Dumek was attacked by a wolf near the village of Loanezi in Croatia. She was saved by some of her cattle which assaulted the wolf. She was expected to survive and the report attributed this to divine providence. Whether this was also the belief of the English journalist is unknown.

4 April 1836
A Negro man in Liberty Valley, Perry County, USA, was eaten by wolves on an unspecified day in the previous week. The source of this information was the *Juniata Journal.*

6 February 1838
From *The Journal of Grenoble.* A wolf attacked a group of sixteen or seventeen

peasants from the village of Aves near the bridge of Vareille on the river Egburan. This occurred on 30th January sometime after 22:00.

30 November 1844
A labourer fought a wolf at Chenevry and managed to escape.

21 February 1845
A French cowherd managed to scare off wolves by beating his shoes together.

26 March 1845
Two women and an infant were killed by a wolf at Genestons. They were returning from the baby's christening with their husbands who lingered in the pub and found the bodies on their way home. No names are mentioned and this would seem to be an apocryphal tale about the dangers of neglecting family in favour of alcohol.

16 October 1846
There was a wolf hunt at St-Laurent-en-Caux which resulted in a huntsman being injured.

31 January 1848
A letter from a town on the river Doubs said that a child of eight was carried off by a wolf. The body was not found.

16 August 1852
A mad wolf was described in a letter from Smyrna, now Izimir in modern Turkey. No precise date of the incident is given but the letter is dated 26 July. The wolf wounded 128 people, killed 85 sheep and wounded 75 more in just one day. The numbers seem exaggerated and the animal was probably rabid. This suspicion is strengthened by the fact that none of the victims were eaten.

This is similar to a case identified by Linnell's team, involving a rabid wolf in Lorges Forest, France on 25 April 1851. The wolf travelled 45 kilometres through nine villages in seven hours. It bit 41 people, nineteen of whom were children, and 96 animals. Fourteen of the people bitten were confirmed dead within two months (Linnell 2002: 20). It may be the same case mentioned in *The Times*.

30 March 1853
A priest and twenty-one parishioners at Ola Pian near Mulhlbach in Transylvania were bitten by a mad wolf while leaving a church. Twelve died. Transylvania is famous for the werewolf although this owes more to confusion between vampires and werewolves than any local lycanthropy myths. Again rabies is a likely explanation for the behaviour of the wolf.

28 November 1856
A letter from Warsaw said that there were a lot of wolves in that area. One entered the village of Szymanow in daylight and carried off a six-year-old child. This story was criticised by the zoologist Erik Zimen who said that it would require a very large wolf and a very small child (Zimen 1980: 328–9). The information is at least second-hand. The child is not named, nor is the letter writer from Warsaw.

23 April 1862
This refers to the death of a man who rescued another man from a wolf in February. It is stated that the death of the first man was reported in *The Times* at the time, but I was unable to trace this.

1 May 1863
Monsieur Decheppe was pursued through a forest by two wolves but stayed calm and was unharmed. There are elements of the folk tale about this report and it is by no means clear that the wolves intended to harm the man.

1 December 1863
Two young ladies in Canada encountered an aggressive wolf. On 10 May 1890 *The Times* would refer to Canadian wolves as not being aggressive.

20 January 1856
This describes a wolf attack at a place between Nantes and St. Jean-de-Bruel. A man and a girl were reported killed from injuries sustained in the fight. The wolf was described as being of gigantic size.

12 October 1874
From the Paris correspondent of the *Pall Mall Gazette*. A wolf killed a little girl, Marie Favrand in Charente as she was picking chestnuts. It then attacked a man named Texier, who sustained twenty-two wounds as he tried to rescue her. He was assisted by another man, Fontronbande, who had his finger lacerated.

24 August 1876
This describes an appendix to an official report published in St Petersburg which contained statistics about wolves in Russia. There is one story of a peasant who found a wolf that was pretending to be dead. He took it home for the pelt and was killed. The report stated that two hundred people were killed by wolves in Russia in 1873. This seems a high figure considering that Linnell identified 273 victims in a twenty-one year period between 1840 and 1861.

24 April 1877
A man and his family were travelling along the banks of the River Pruth in Prussia on a sleigh pursed by wolves. To deter them the peasant threw off his children one by one. His wife informed the authorities but they acquitted him of murder. Stories of children being thrown from sleighs to wolves, or other animals, often occur in fiction. Wolves would chase sleighs due to the rushing stimulus of the horses. Experiments with rabbits and rodents have demonstrated that wolves refrain from attacking prey until it moves. The stimulus of a rushing creature is required to provoke a reaction. This is true of many other animals. Flight is a reaction which the predator associates with fear and potential prey species. Sudden movement is inadvisable when confronted with any potentially dangerous animal.

Given the ability of wolves to read the body language of their prey there may be a case of cause and effect in that fear displayed, consciously or not, by humans provokes the wolf. The natural response for someone taught to fear wolves is to run away from them. Pursuit is the natural response for a wolf, or any other predator, when confronted by something fleeing.

Erkki Pulliainen reported that if a wolf and a human met in Finland then the wolf would step aside (Pulliainen 1979: 90). If the person had showed fear first then the reaction might have been different. Wolves coming into contact with people have been known to urinate and defecate which are symptoms of fear in many species, including humans. The existence of two species which mistrust each other creates a climate for mutual aggression. Teaching people to fear the wolf may therefore place them in danger.

21 June 1877
This quotes an official report saying that there were 200,000 wolves in European Russia which had caused the deaths of 161 people in 1875 and an average of 125 between 1849 and 1851. Again this is much higher than Linnell's figures but it was accepted by a number of later writers. An article in the science journal *Nature* repeats the figure in 1933, citing Lydekker as the authority (Anon. 1933). Richard Lydekker's book *Royal Natural History* was published in 1894.

29 November 1877
A mad wolf was killed near Brittany in France after attacking ten people. Three children died.

16 January 1878
A postman was attacked by a wolf in the Lorraine region.

8 January 1880
A girl was devoured by a wolf while shut in a barn at Baud in France.

6 February 1880
This cites *The Cologne Gazette* which stated that wolves were getting bold in Finland. They were attacking sleighs and ate an eight-year old child. In this report we have an English newspaper citing a German newspaper as evidence of events in Finland.

19 July 1883
This article discusses the cost of wolf depredation in European Russia, repeating the figure of 161 people killed by wolves in 1875.

2 August 1884
This refers to a French law passed two years earlier which increased the bounties on wolves, with the interesting comment that this has increased the efficiency of officials. It implies that people had no motivation to destroy wolves before rewards were offered and therefore that they did not consider wolves to be a danger to them. Eight pounds was paid for the destruction of wolves that had attacked people and nine such wolves were killed the previous year in three of the central districts of France. It was not clear how the attacks were verified.

21 November 1884

A Hungarian priest was travelling by sledge to Lonka with his pregnant wife and child when they were attacked by twenty wolves which killed him and the boy. His wife miscarried and died shortly afterwards. Despite the fatal injury she managed to give a good account of the incident. Packs of twenty wolves are uncommon which suggests an exaggeration, especially as she escaped. We are informed that the priest had a parish at Krasnisora.

22 January 1888

This states that wolves were eating people in Hungary and gives two examples. One was a magistrate who fell from a sleigh and the other was a boy thrown from a sleigh by his father who wished to evade the wolves himself. The bereaved parent surrendered himself to police.

26 December 1888

This gives figures of wolves killed in France. Two of the 701 killed in 1887 had attacked humans. This is a low attack ratio, especially when rabies is considered. It is also significant as larger bounties were paid for wolves which had attacked humans so one would expect a number of false claims or exaggerations.

5 November 1890

This cites information from unnamed Indian papers. The bounty offered was 25 rupees for a wolf and 300 for a pack. These rewards follow reports that the Hoshangabad district in Central Province was being targeted by eight wolves which had killed forty cattle watchers, aged between eight and sixteen, but left the cattle untouched.

**Modern reports of wolves attacking humans**

Since the nineteenth century the mechanism for reporting attacks by wolves on people has greatly improved. In the twentieth century more people are known to have been killed by wolves in India than in any other country. Before looking at some of theses incidents it is worth considering one unconfirmed story of a wolf attack in Iran. The attack took place in May 1997 and was summarised in the May 1998 edition of *Fortean Times* as follows. In the countryside around Leig a hungry wolf entered a house and tried to eat a 25-year old man. His mother Setareh Safari, aged 65, witnessed the incident and strangled the wolf. Mother and son were treated in Behbahan hospital. Linnell noted that this report was unconfirmed (Linnell 2002: 57). although the *Fortean Times* report credits an Iranian journal, *Jomhuri Islami*. Interestingly the next notice on the *Fortean Times* Web site describes a cow in Iran eating a child.

**Wolves attacking humans in India**

The Iranian wolf, *Canis lupus palipes,* is a subspecies of wolf distinct from *Canis lupus lupus,* and studies of its behaviour cannot be used to explain the behaviour of *Canis lupus lupus.* There are several differences between the two. For example *Canis lupus palipes* preys by surprise attack while *Canis lupus lupus* preys by giving chase.

*Canis lupus palipes* lives in pairs or family packs and does not howl but *Canis lupus lupus* lives, for the most part, in packs and does howl.

*Canis lupus palipes* is indigenous to India and other parts of Asia. This Indian wolf differs in appearance from the European wolf, being smaller and more like a jackal.

Blaine wrote of it:

> The Indian wolf bears the same wolfish character which belongs to his European congeners. He is a sly lurking assassin, ready to murder children at all times and sometimes if he can get a little help, he will attack a man. A woman is by no means safe in the sight of a single hungry wolf. (Blaine 1800 (1852: 33))

Stories of the Indian wolf eating children have been circulating in England for approximately 150 years. William Ireland believed that wolves killed more people per year than other predators in India, stating that five to six thousand children per annum were killed, with three to four hundred of them in Oude (Ireland 1900: 437). Apparently there were annual statistics collated in some Indian provinces of fatalities caused by wild beasts. Such lists do not appear to have survived. They supposedly included fatalities caused by snake bite and no attempt was made to compile separate lists for separate predators. Despite these deficiencies Jim Corbett felt that the procedures for establishing deaths caused by predators in India were reasonably accurate in the early twentieth century (Corbett 1954: 7–8). No evidence has been located to support Ireland's statistics and it is unlikely that the deaths of six thousand children per year would go unnoticed in other records.

Linnell and his team identified a large number of predatory attacks by wolves on humans in India during the twentieth century. These were concentrated in three states. In the Hazaribagh region of Bihar state at least two hundred children were killed by wolves between 1980 and 1995. In the Eastern region of Uttar Pradesh state fifty children were killed by wolves in 1996 and further attacks followed over the next three years. In the Antantpur region of Andhra Pradesh nine children were killed between 1980 and 1981.

Biologists Yadavendradev Jhala and Dinesh Sharma investigated the 1996 incident and identified one wolf responsible for two deaths (Bishop 1998). Later research suggested that a pack was involved and that fifty children died in 76 attacks (Linnell 2002: 26). On average the attacks occurred every third day between March and October, with an average reported death every five days. Victims were aged between four months and nine years, with death resulting from fatal bites to the throat. The total area covered was 450 square miles. Features of this area included a high density of livestock, a low population of the wolf's natural prey and large numbers of unescorted children.

The story was reported in the West, most notably in the *New York Times* on the 1 September 1996, which named one of the victims as four year old Anand Kumar from Banbirpur. This report stated that 33 children had been killed and 20 injured in five months, according to police figures. It also said that British officials in 1878 catalogued 624 deaths caused by wolves in India. At least one Indian source reported further deaths and attacks in the area around Rae Bareilly between 2000 and 2001 (NDTV Correspondent 2001).

In 1996 the Indian authorities issued new guidelines to people living in areas where wolf attacks were reported. These stated that children were not to be left unsupervised and advised greater diligence. It also concluded that the behaviour of the wolves was abnormal. This distinction was understood in Europe in earlier times but the causes of the aberrations were not.

One explanation for the Indian attacks was that over-hunting by people had decimated the normal prey species of wolves, forcing them to attack livestock. This brought them closer to human communities and children often had less protection than the livestock. Small children were also easier to catch, especially for a single wolf. Were attacks like these common when conditions in Europe mirrored those now found in India?

### Contemporary opinions on wolves eating people

Question eight of the survey asked if wolves eat people. 184 respondents answered this question as follows:

| Answer | Number of replies |
| --- | --- |
| No | 93 |
| Yes | 40 |
| Sometimes | 26 |
| Possibly | 22 |
| Don't know | 2 |

Of those who committed themselves to a definite yes or no answer more than two-thirds answered no. However fifty-two of the respondents were unsure, suggesting that they would benefit from education about wolves.

Question nine asked if wolves were dangerous to people. The answers of the 186 respondents who replied were as follows:

| Answer | Number of Replies |
| --- | --- |
| Yes | 62 |
| No | 58 |
| Possibly | 36 |
| Sometimes | 31 |
| Don't know | 2 |

A third of the respondents felt that wolves were dangerous to people.

## A wolf-attack in Canada

On 8 November 2005 the body of a twenty-two year old man was found at Points North Landing near Wollaston Lake in the Canadian province of Saskatchewan. A pack of four wolves were suspected as being the cause of his death. Two were shot and found to have cloth and hair in the large intestine that was then sent for analysis to confirm if it was of human origin. If this incident is confirmed as a wolf attack it will be the first recorded instance of a healthy wild wolf attacking a person in North America and a rare instance in which a pack of wolves were involved in the death of a person. This wolf pack had become accustomed to humans; they fed on garbage and may have associated people with food.

Possible reasons why wolves might eat people include a lack of natural prey, a high wolf population, a human community without firearms and wolves that were used to scavenging on corpses. All of these criteria were more likely to have existed simultaneously in the past than today. In addition today's humans generally live in communities that are less vulnerable and have better protection while the worldwide wolf population is much lower than in previous times. Some rural parts of India still report wolf attacks in conditions that are similar to those in nineteenth century Europe. Despite this there is no evidence to suggest that wolf attacks on humans were, or are, commonplace. Interestingly wolves in India are not feared in the same way as they are in Europe and North America where the number of verified instances is disproportionate to the fear. So it is appropriate to look next at some of the reasons for that fear.

# Chapter three

# The Devil Wolf

Since ancient times the comparison between bellicose wolf and passive lamb has been used in literature as a metaphor of good and evil, or strength and weakness. Herodotus wrote: 'Theras's son refused to accompany the expedition and Theras said he would be leaving him behind like a sheep among wolves; the remark caught on.' (Herodotus (1996 4.19)) In this quotation the connotation of the wolf is positive and the sheep is associated with cowardice. Later, especially in Christian cultures, wolves were given negative connotations.

Several variants of the wolf and lamb metaphor appear in the Old Testament. Sirach asks: 'What fellowship has a wolf with a lamb? No more has a sinner with a godly man.' (*Sirach* 13.17) He is not suggesting that the wolf is evil; just making a comparison that would have been familiar to his audience. The wolf's ferocity and cruelty are noted in Genesis and Ezekiel while Zephaniah associates the wolf with the night (*Genesis* 49.25; *Ezekiel* 22.27; *Zephaniah* 3.3).

Evil connotations of the wolf are found in the New Testament, expanding on the ferocity and cruelty examples. John the Evangelist recites the tale of a shepherd who abandoned his flock to flee from a wolf (*John* 10: 12–13). This wolf is symbolic of evil or danger coming from outside. The parable may have been intended to foreshadow Jesus' trial and subsequent dispersal of his disciples.

In Matthew's gospel Jesus refers to wolves twice. He calls false prophets 'ferocious wolves' and tells his disciples that he is sending them out as sheep amongst wolves (*Matthew* 7.15, 10.16). The idea presented is that the world around is full of evil just as the woods are full of wolves. Here wolves are associated with treachery, a connotation more commonly afforded to foxes.

In the Acts of the Apostles Paul warns that savage wolves, alias false prophets, would come amongst the Ephesians (*Acts* 20.29). Again Christ's followers are compared to sheep and the rest of the hostile world to wolves. The analogy is included to make a point about the vulnerability of the new believers. This is not developed further but firmly denotes the wolf as an external threat.

In the New Testament the wolf was occasionally used as a symbol of the evil that faced, or was expected to face, the followers of Christ. Wolves were not portrayed as inherently evil. Early Christianity did not credit animals with free will, regarding them as being created by God for specific purposes. Yet the place of the wolf in the divine plan was not always obvious and the activities of wolves were detrimental to human interests. An animal that people were unable to control appeared incongruous, especially as God had given humans control over their environment.

Theologians put forward two reasons to account for the presence of wolves. Firstly wild beasts were seen as instruments of divine punishment to be utilised by God as he saw fit. Secondly the Fall of Man was considered responsible. Both ideas are connected in the sense that they see wild beasts as punishment for sins. The first sees this punishment as being controlled by God in response to specific individual or group sins, and the second considers it to be a more arbitrary process for which Adam and Eve were originally responsible. The first idea helped shape Christian perceptions of the wolf.

## Wolves are punishments sent by God

The idea of wolves punishing people who had offended deities appears in classical literature. Herodotus tells how Evenuis fell asleep while guarding sheep and the flock was then destroyed by wolves (Herodotus: 9.93). In another ancient story, related by Pausanias, Gelanor resigned the leadership of Argos in favour of Danaus after a wolf attacked and killed a bull. (Pausanias (1979 Vol.1: 175)) The wolf was thought to have been Apollo in disguise, or at least to have been sent by Apollo. Danaus therefore dedicated a shrine to the god. This is similar to a tale of Aelian's (Aelian: 13.1). The wolf has no individual characteristics in Pausanias's story and is presented as a servant of the divine power. This role could presumably have been filled by any large predator.

Aelian gives three examples of the wolf being used as an instrument of divine providence. In the first a wolf leads priests to booty stolen from a temple. In the second two men seeking the right marriage asked the oracle at Delphi for advice. They were instructed to look in the area where they found the fiercest animal carrying the gentlest. This turned out to be a wolf bearing a lamb at Cleonae, which is seven or eight miles south-west of Corinth. In the third story a wolf ran into a schoolroom and stole the writing tablet of Gelon of Syracuse (*circa* 578–540 BC). Gelon gave pursuit and the classroom collapsed behind him, killing everyone else. Aelian comments on the strangeness of a wolf saving a man's life rather than killing him. Clearly he was aware of a belief in wolves that killed people but does not give details.

Early Christian writers had to explain why their benevolent deity allowed wolves to steal the sheep of his followers and permitted the occurrence of natural disasters. Satan and his servants would later take the blame for these occurrences, but in early Christianity there was no clear concept of Satan. Attempts were made to solve this problem by referring back to the Old Testament where God was often described as using his power to punish as well as reward. According to the first *Book of Kings*: 'The Lord brings evil on them for forsaking the God.' (1 *Kings* 9. 9–10) Several other biblical stories describe God punishing sinners. The message was clear. Those who broke the religious code, which also served as a political and social code would be punished by God. The threat of such punishment was intended to be a deterrent.

For a deterrent to influence people it needs to be visible. The successes of human enemies and destructive behaviour of wild animals were effective literary representations of divine wrath. Isaiah states that the Assyrians were sent as punishment for sinners. *Deuteronomy* uses the threat of wild beasts and Jeremiah specifies the wolf, along with the lion and the leopard (*Isaiah* 10.5; *Deuteronomy* 32.24; *Jeremiah* 5.6). Wolves are not singled out for individual attention. God was thought to control all animals and could therefore employ them as he saw fit, without distinguishing between species.

Divine punishment was also described as the cause of natural disasters. The second book of *Maccabees* reads: 'Now I urge those who read this book not to be despaired by such calamities but to recognise that these punishments were designed not to destroy but to discipline our people.' (2 *Maccabees* 6.12) The earliest biblical story in which a natural disaster is attributed to God is the flood of Noah. Another famous example is the ten plagues of Egypt. Three of the plagues involved insects and another involved frogs.

Natural disasters were described in Matthew's gospel as omens preceding the end of the world. (*Matthew* 24: 7-8) In *Revelation* death is described as having the power to kill by sword, famine, plague and wild beasts, although the species are not specified. (*Revelation* 7.8) This concept would inspire many later Christian writers who sought to explain events around them by referring to incidents and speeches from the Bible.

The influence and longevity of this concept is evinced by the comments of the Bishop of Metz on New Year's Eve in 1764. Referring to the beast of Gevaudan he quoted *Leviticus*: 'I will let loose the wild beasts among you, which will rob you of your children, and destroy your cattle and make you few in number so that your ways become desolate.' (*Leviticus* 26.22; Thompson 1991: 69–76) · By portraying the activities of the beast as divine punishment the Bishop probably hoped to increase religious observance in the area.

Events such as meteorite showers, strong winds, storms and fires were often viewed as examples of divine wrath. These were unpredictable and damaging occurrences that might make people think that God was failing them. Sometimes they would be described as a prelude to worse disasters. The intention was that worried sinners would be prompted to repent. Wolves were placed in this category of natural disasters. The loss of livestock to wolves could be substantial and raids by wolves were unpredictable. Farmers had much to fear when they heard wolves howling in the distance. This fear could be exploited.

### Examples of the wolf as omen

There are examples of benevolent wolves in early Christian literature but evil connotations are also found. Orosius's *Histories against the Pagans* was held in high regard throughout mediaeval Christendom and was translated into Anglo-Saxon at King Alfred's request as one of the six books that were most necessary for all men to know. In this book *Orosius* describes an omen when three wolves brought a body into Rome and tore it to pieces (Thorpe 1857: 4.2). From this early time the wolf was associated with death and destruction.

Other Christian writers incorporated the idea of the wolf as an omen into their anecdotes and morality tales. Gregory of Tours, writing toward the end of the sixth century told how a city was threatened by portents which included earthquakes, and stags and wolves entering the city. On the night of the Easter Vigil the royal palace started to burn. The bishop prayed for mercy and afterwards extinguished the flames with his tears. Thereafter he was able to supervise repentance (Gregory of Tours (1927: 8.33)). Gregory also tells how a wolf came into Poitiers through one of the gates and was killed within the city walls (Gregory of Tours (1927: 5.13)). From this we may infer that wolves were thought to belong outside the city, just as evil belonged outside Christianity. This idea persisted for some time. Serious trouble lay ahead when the sanctuary was breached. Yet, even then, there remained enough time to slay the intruder. This is in keeping with the Christian message that it is never too late to repent.

Gregory's third story featuring wolves tells how a group of them entered Bordeaux and devoured some dogs (Gregory of Tours (1927: 6.14)) This is symbolic of the unknown wilderness conquering the known and again indicates a lack of safety in places previously regarded as secure. It is a warning against complacency.

Numerous references to Gregory and Orosius in later texts indicate the influence that they had on their successors. Neither portrays wolves as consciously evil but in their stories it is a symbol of danger without being directly dangerous in itself. Always it is an external threat, entering and causing problems in previously safe environments.

## Associations between the wolf and evil people

As Christianity developed enemies of the faith were described as wolves with the wolf/lamb and Christ as lamb metaphors. Æthelfrith, king of Northumbria who died in 616, behaved like a wolf according to Bede (Bede 1.34). By this time a series of characteristics were associated with the wolf so humans displaying these characteristics could be called wolves. There are no extant sources detailing what the characteristics were but greed and rapacity must have been among them.

Associating wolves with violent groups encouraged people to view wolves in a negative manner. The Vikings are the most noteworthy example. From the end of the eighth century onwards their raids on Francia, England and Ireland increased in frequency and some of the raiders settled in various parts of eastern and north-western Britain. Christian annalists portrayed the presence and activities of the Vikings as God's judgment on sinners. In some cases they described the Vikings as wolves. This comparison firmly established the evil connotations of wolves.

## The Vikings as wolves

In 793 a group of Scandinavians attacked a monastery at Lindisfarne, off the coast of Northumbria. Although it was by no means the first Viking raid on western Europe it is generally considered by historians to mark the start of the first Viking period. The incident was recorded in the *Anglo-Saxon Chronicles* as follows:

> In this year dire portents appeared over Northumbria and sorely frightened the people. They consisted of immense whirlwinds, and flashes of lightning and fiery dragons were seen flying through the air. A great famine immediately followed these signs; and a little after that in the same year, on 8 January [the raid actually took place in June] the ravages of heathen men miserably destroyed God's church on Lindisfarne with plunder and slaughter.

The portents, presumably invented or exaggerated, were used by the annalist to foreshadow the raid. The idea of savage Vikings attacking Christians for religious, rather than economic reasons was challenged in Peter Sawyer's *The Age of the Vikings*, in 1962. Sawyer considered the activities of the Vikings to be an extension of Dark Age trading activities rather than atrocities motivated by a hatred of Christianity. The traditional view is based on an acceptance of the extant sources as more or less accurate records of events while Sawyer's revisionist theory claims that the sources were biased and therefore inaccurate. A balanced view would be that the Vikings were plunderers with little or no respect for the Christian religion but were not motivated by religious hatred.

This view was not shared by the contemporary chroniclers who recorded the raids. The principal sources are the Frankish *Annals of St Bertin* and *Annals of Fulda*. Both were probably known in England as King Alfred (840–900) recruited Frankish scholars who would have brought books and information with them. The main English sources for this topic are *The Anglo-Saxon Chronicles* and Asser's *Life of King Alfred*.

*The Anglo-Saxon Chronicles* are known to have been in circulation from 892 onwards; they were maintained and added to until the middle of the twelfth century. There were several regional independent versions that later scholars merged into one more-or-less continuous text. Asser's *Life of King Alfred* was written by the Bishop of Sherborne towards the end of the eponymous King's reign. This is a short and confusing text that may not have been fully completed. Along with the *Anglo-Saxon Chronicles*, it was probably commissioned by Alfred as part of his drive to increase learning. Alfred believed that Christianity was in decline and blamed this on ignorance as explicitly stated in the preface to his translation of Gregory's *Pastoral Care*. He was so concerned by the lack of learning that he organised translations of several important theological works into the vernacular. This constitutes important evidence that there was at least a perceived decline in Christianity in England prior to the arrival of the Vikings. Alfred believed that the Vikings were sent by God as punishment for the sins of the Christians and conveyed this message in the literature which he commissioned.

In several entries the *Anglo-Saxon Chronicles* makes it clear that the battle against the Vikings is not merely groups of the English fighting parties of Scandinavians, but the Christians battling against the pagans. At that time there was no real sense of national identity and one of Alfred's triumphs lay in unifying some of the country. A belief in Christianity and the impact of the Viking raids were factors that the different regions of England had in common. The *Anglo-Saxon Chronicles* record the progress of the Viking army in England, culminating in Alfred's victory over them. But it is not just a story of the English king beating the foreigners. It is the story of Christianity defeating paganism and overcoming evil. The public baptism of the Danish leader Gunthrum is the ultimate spiritual triumph. The influence of this display on the watching populace must have been, and was surely intended to be, hugely significant.

Asser's *Life of King Alfred* copies the *Anglo-Saxon Chronicle* from 851–87, the period of the most intense Viking pressure. Earlier he tells how King Ethelred delayed a battle to hear mass. He also relates how the Christians were divinely inspired to win a particular battle against the odds. In another anecdote he speaks of divine providence in telling how villains were thwarted in their plans to attack a priest. Asser's text may not have the literary sophistication of the Frankish annals but it is designed to portray the Christian God as supreme and those who follow him as successful.

There were real military reasons to oppose the Vikings and assumed spiritual reasons to do so. By combining the two the Frankish annalists hoped to strengthen that opposition and the faith of the laity. In England during the ninth century Christianity was also viewed as a means of uniting different groups, a role it once fulfilled in the Roman Empire. The annals are not necessarily accurate records of events, they were written for a specific purpose and their writers made extensive use of symbolism to make specific points. The wolf was one of the metaphors adopted.

### Symbolic use of the wolf in anti-Viking texts

Asser only once refers to the Vikings as wolves, in his seventy-eighth chapter. Elsewhere he describes them as crafty foxes when they broke a treaty. This further indicates that wolves had no specific role of their own within Christian thought at that time. Nonetheless some ninth century church leaders linked wolves to evil. In 886 Fulco, Bishop of Rheims, wrote a letter to Alfred in which he described the Vikings as visible wolves. Unhappy with some priests sent by the English king Fulco wrote: 'For you have sent to me some dogs, which though well-bred and excellent, yet corporeal and mortal are intended for driving away the fury of visible wolves, with which among other scourges sent to us through God's just judgment for our country greatly abounds.' (Keynes and Lapidge 1983: 184) This letter indicates that, in line with earlier precedents, wolves were firmly associated with external threats.

The Frankish annals make several references to wolves. The entry for the year 846 in the *Annals of St Bertin* states that wolves devoured the inhabitants of western Gaul and marched in army formations of three hundred. It is made explicitly clear that the wolves were Danish pirates. To complete the tale of woe the annalist describes a terribly fierce wind lasting the whole winter. The forces of nature were again associated with divine punishment.

Another story is told in the *Annals of Fulda*, for the year 850. It relates how a man set out with his wife and small child in search of food. On the journey he suggested that they eat the boy. His wife refused to allow this but he seized the boy and would have slain him if he had not seen two wolves killing a deer. He promptly drove away the wolves and stole their meal. The role of the wolves in this story is as divine guides, just as it is in the St Edmund story related by Abbo of Fluery. This tenth century life of the saint describes how he was martyred by the Vikings and how a wolf guided searchers to his severed head (Arnold 1870: 18–19). Perhaps the point being made is that the Vikings were worse than wolves in their atrocities. Abbo claimed to have received his information from St Edmund's standard bearer, but the only surviving near-contemporary report of Edmund's death is a line in the *Anglo Saxon Chronicle* for 870, which notes that the Danes killed the king. Abbo's claim of veracity is undermined by his usage of motifs borrowed from classical sources. This particular story may derive from one by the Greek writer Pausanias who said that a wolf killed a man who had been plundering wealth then guided searchers to the spot where the treasure was hidden (Pausanias (1979 Vol.1: 443)).

The entry for the year 858 in the *Annals of St Bertin*, demonstrates thematically the process of natural order being overthrown. In sequence it describes: an earthquake, a great pestilence, a tree being thrown up by the sea, a wolf running around the church of St Porcaria in the Sens district, the death of the Saxon king Æthelwulf (the noble wolf), the ransoming of material from churches, the defection of the king's court, the handing over of the kingdom to the king's brother Lothar, a flood, a Viking attack, Lothar's imprisoning his wife, the desertion of the king's men and the return of a monk with relics. This is no random sequence of events. Every paragraph relates to the selected theme, including some presumably invented for the purpose, such as the washed-up tree and the wolf. With this story the annalist probably intended to warn sinners that they were not safe, even in church. The wolf came from outside, penetrating the perceived sanctuary. There is an entry in the *Motif-Index of Folk-Literature*, involving a wolf inside a church (Thompson 1966: Q454.4). The presence of a wolf inside a church had also been noted in the *Annals of St Bertin* the previous year. This was at Trier and is similar to a much later story concerning the supposed appearance of a black dog at St Mary's church at Bungay, Suffolk, in August 1577. That incident was described in a contemporary pamphlet by Alexander Flemming. As a puritan writing at a time of religious unrest Flemming had good reason to exaggerate the effects of divine punishment. There is no mention of a dog in any other near-contemporary account of the incident, not even in the churchwarden's books for St Mary's. Flemming was responsible for translating a pamphlet on English dogs the previous year and was familiar with folklore motifs featuring dogs as instruments of divine punishment. His work shows that in the sixteenth century natural disasters were commonly viewed as God's punishment on sinners.

The similarities between the incidents in Trier and Bungay are important for three reasons. Firstly the fact that *the Annals of St Bertin* describe a wolf in a church as an omen and nearly six centuries later Flemming tells a similar story about a dog instead of a wolf, indicates that canids are interchangeable in tales of this kind. Secondly it suggests that *the Annals of St Bertin* or other versions of the motif were known in sixteenth century England and thirdly it demonstrates that some historical sources repeat earlier accounts. This repetition reinforced and strengthened established beliefs.

The Frankish annals contain several descriptions of divine punishment for people who were sinful. In their accounts of such incidents the annals deny their classification as a record of chronological events. They appear more as a blend of real and imaginary occurrences, twisted to satisfy a preconceived theme. They stress the merits of living as a good Christian and describe the punishments that fall on those who fail.

## Propaganda?

Whether the Vikings threatened the church or not, it was expedient for church leaders to claim that they did. Fear became the driving force as the church sought to assert itself. Clerics were faced with the dilemma of persuading the laity that God was the powerful deity when natural disasters and the Vikings were disrupting normal life. One method was to suggest that these events were punishments for sins and that reformed behaviour would remove them.

By portraying the Vikings as divine punishment and exaggerating their impact Christian writers hoped to raise the profile of Christianity among an indolent laity and ensure future obedience. This is the same principle used in the Old Testament of describing divine punishment as a deterrent. Wolves were valuable symbols in the propaganda exercise undertaken by the annalists.

The association made between wolves and Vikings may seem insignificant. There is no evidence that the metaphor was widely disseminated or that it inspired Christian aggression against either the wolf or the Scandinavians. Yet it is important as this is the first time that the wolf was consistently associated with a specific, visible evil and portrayed as an enemy of Christianity by several sources. From this time forward benevolent connotations of wolves are less often found and malevolent ones become more common.

## Links between the wolf and Satan

In 1014 Archbishop Wulfstan preached the famous sermon of the wolf to the English, using the pseudonym Lupus. In this he talked about divine retribution. When natural disasters were presented by clergymen as divine punishment there was little that the populace could do, except repent their sins. The ideology of the Church gradually changed. Instead of persuading people to reform through fear of divine punishment, the clerical authorities began punishing those who they considered to be spiritually deficient. The visual deterrent of this punishment was intended to ensure future compliance in both social and religious terms. A crucial development was the emergence of Satan in Christian thought.

Prior to the early middle ages the Devil was usually described, in theological and lay sources, as a comical figure who invariably lost to the forces of God. The growth of a belief in a powerful source of evil, referred to as Satan, was related to the growth in the church's political and social power. Previously, with a precarious official position that often depended on royal patronage and a laity who were not committed, the Church could not afford to acknowledge the existence of a powerful rival to God. Then it seemed more appropriate to portray natural disasters as divine punishment to emphasise the power of God and persuade people to obey rather than force them to do so.

In 1215 the following was decreed at the fourth Lateran council:

> Lest for the lack of a shepherd a rapacious wolf attack the Lord's flock and a bereaved church suffer grave injury to the good and wishing in this matter to counteract the damage to souls and provide protection for churches we decree that a cathedral or monastery may not be without a prelate for more than three months.

(Douglas and Greenway 1961: 55)

In adopting the wolf-lamb metaphor and portraying the enemies of Christ as wolves the clergy were helping to persuade the laity that wolves were evil.

As literature and theology became more sophisticated, Christian writers increasingly portrayed wolves as evil rather than merely as a symbol of evil or an instrument of God. Wolves would be further associated with Satan who became recognised, and feared, by church leaders as the controlling intelligence behind all evil. This had not always been the case. The *Motif-Index of Folk-Literature* lists a couple of motifs in which wolves are the enemy of the Devil (Thompson 1966: G303.25.1 and G303.17.3.3). Nevertheless by the tenth century Christian writers most commonly depicted the wolf as evil.

In the eleventh century life of St Maieul of Cluny (died 951), also known as Majolus, wolves were described as being extremely ferocious in areas which the Saracens would later attack (Herilhy 1971: 17–18). One wolf was described as being more dangerous than the others, probably representing Satan among his disciples. A man named Folcher, father of Maieul, ordered fences to be erected and pens to be created for the goats, sheep and lambs. Because of the ferocity of the wolves nobody had dared to do this before. Then Folcher began to spend the night close to the sheepfold. Soon the wolves attacked. The cruellest one was unable to pierce Folcher's armour. The knight seized him by the feet, took him to his comrades and imprisoned him for a day prior to destroying him. In his bowels they found whole limbs of human beings. After his death all other wolves fled the land.

The writer of St Maieul's life believed that the aggressive wolves foretold the coming of the Saracens and that the actions of Folcher foreshadowed the achievements of his saintly son. Interestingly, the wolves are portrayed as being of exceptional ferocity, further indication that man-eating was viewed as an abnormal trait. Another feature of this tale is the individualisation of the chief wolf. Wolves were no longer portrayed as being the same and this allowed Satan, and humans, to be personified in wolf form.

## The Bestiary

The evil image of the wolf was widely disseminated through the various bestiaries. These were derived from *The Physiologus*, a Greek text written around AD 200 but probably based on earlier sources. Mediaeval bestiaries included descriptions and illustrations of a variety of real and mythical animals. There were around forty animals in the original with later versions including anything from twelve to one hundred. A typical entry begins with an etymological explanation of the animal's name then proceeds to describe its physical characteristics and behavioural traits. A moral concludes the description.

Visual and oral sources tend to be much more influential in shaping people's perceptions of the wolf than written ones. Since bestiaries were accompanied by illustrations they were able to influence many more people than exclusively written sources, especially in a period when literacy levels were low.

The Bestiary of Bishop Theobald (*circa* 1022–45), included twelve creatures – lion, eagle, snake, ant, fox, stag, spider, whale, siren, elephant, turtle-dove and panther. One use of this bestiary, explained by the author, was to teach Christians to avoid vices such as pride, avarice, gluttony and luxury, thereby rousing them to the virtues of prudence, justice, temperance and fortitude.

The author advises us that the Devil is represented by the nature of the fox. In other bestiaries the fox is also shown as deceitful, feigning death to catch prey. Notably, the behaviour of Reynard the Fox is often worse than that of the wolf Isengrim, being treacherous, cunning and malevolent. Possibly the later evil image of the wolf is derived, in part, from the image of the fox. Certainly there are similarities as the fox was also a threat to farmers and a more potent one in England.

Richard de Fournival's French bestiary of the mid-thirteenth century seeks metaphors of animals and love. He refers to Pliny's statement that the man or wolf makes the other dumb, believing that this happens when lovers meet. Further, he compared the wolf's inability to bend its neck with the female habit of giving themselves completely. The fact that the wolf hunted prey away from its den was similar to women loving from a distance and the wolf's willingness to bite its own foot was compared to women protecting themselves (Beer 1986: 4–5).

Not all the carnivorous animals in this bestiary are depicted as evil. The lion destroying other animals is compared by Theobald to Christ destroying sinners. Again we see the theme of divine retribution. Christ is also represented as the panther. Other writers depict the lion and leopard, or panther, as evil. Dante describes these two beasts and a she-wolf obstructing a path (Dante 1984: 1265–1321). There was no consensus of opinion. Perhaps bestiary writers felt able to bestow positive connotations on the lion and panther because these were animals that would not be familiar to their audiences. The wolf and the fox threatened livestock and therefore had no place in the world which God had created for humans.

The account of the wolf, *De Lupo*, was a tenth century addition to *The Physiologus* which does not appear in all bestiary manuscripts. By the twelfth century however some bestiaries disseminated in England did contain a description of the wolf. Richard Barber translated a typical example (Barber 1992: 69–71). The wolf was said to have derived its name from the Greek, *likos*, which came from the word for 'biting' as hungry wolves killed everything that they found. Alternatively it was claimed that the word came from the Greek, *leopos*, meaning 'lion-footed' because their strength was in their feet.

The relevant points are summarised below, with some commentary.

*1. Wolves massacre anyone who passes by*
It is difficult to ascertain where this belief comes from. No earlier sources describing the wolf as habitually dangerous to humans have been found.

*2. Prostitutes are called wolves*
The author notes that whores were called she-wolves because they destroyed the wealth of their lover. This may explain the Romulus and Remus story, if it originally described a prostitute discovering the boys. Prostitutes were frowned on by the mediaeval church but still thrived. Again wolves are associated with groups that were considered to be outside of normal society.

*3. The wolf's eyes shine at night*
Our mediaeval ancestors lived in a world without electricity and were frequently unable to find illumination at night. Nocturnal creatures had an advantage over them. The bestiary explains that the wolf's eyes shine at night because the works of the Devil are considered beautiful by dark humans.

*4. If seen by man before it sees him the wolf loses its ferocity and cannot run*
This would seem to contradict the first point. Of Pliny's story about the man being struck dumb by the sight of a wolf, the bestiary writer says that the man should scare away the wolf by beating two stones together. He interpreted this as a sinner using Christ, or the saints, to scare away Satan.

*5. The Devil is a wolf patrolling sheep*
The idea of a dark force patrolling around the Christian sheepfold comes, as discussed earlier, from the Bible. The belief that the wolf was unable to turn its neck backward was taken to mean that Satan never retreats from sin. The strength in the wolf's forequarters and weakness in its hindquarters reminded the writer how Satan had fallen from heaven. Here we see how beliefs about Satan are linked with wolves. The idea that Lucifer was God's servant before he left heaven is a logical development from the assumption that God utilised natural forces to indicate his displeasure. Once it became accepted that God was only a force for good then a being of almost equal power had to be created to explain the existence of evil. For

this Christian writers could use the Bible for inspiration. Isaiah and Ezekiel describe Lucifer falling from heaven, and Jesus is sometimes interpreted as saying that he witnessed the fall (*Luke* 10.18).

*6. Wolves only copulate for twelve days*
This copies Aristotle.

Bestiaries are worthless as records of natural history. They have value as a record of what people believed at the time, or rather what those who produced and distributed them wanted the laity to believe. We do not know if people really accepted the bestiary accounts as true descriptions of animals or not. For many they would have been their only source of information. The bestiaries do not say much on the subject of man-eating wolves but they do present an image of evil wolves. The images that accompanied them were likely to have been very influential in persuading people to accept these evil connotations.

## Visual images of the wolf

Bearing in mind the low levels of literacy in mediaeval England, and indeed Europe, visual material was often used to convey information. We cannot judge the impact of art on cultural impressions of the wolf in previous times, but pictures and other images had the potential to reach large numbers in a way that written sources could not. In more modern times television documentaries about wolves have reached wider audiences than scientific studies.

Visual images of the wolf do not appear to have been common in England. One of the earliest extant examples is on the Bayeux tapestry where wolves are depicted with long tongues licking their front paws. This may suggest that Guido was right to say that wolves devoured people after the Battle of Hastings. Snarling wolves are depicted on label stops on the door and the arches of the church at Deerhurst in Gloucestershire. The symbolism here is unknown although those on the door may indicate that wolves were considered to belong outside.

## Illustrations

Apart from illustrations in the bestiaries there is a lack of known visual images of the wolf in England until the sixteenth and seventeenth centuries. The cover to a 1665 edition of Aesop's *Fables*, drawn by Francis Barlow, shows the wolf between the fox and the boar. It looks more timid than both of them. Woodcuts accompanied many editions of Aesop and were widely disseminated. They appeared as illustrations in their own right and to commemorate occasions such as executions. Often they had religious significance.

The German Reformation saw an increase in anti-Catholic woodcuts and other visual material. Some Lutheran illustrations show the Catholic hierarchy as wolves, including an amusing image of papal wolves being devoured by sheep (Scribner 1994: 166). A woodcut, *circa* 1480, depicts a Dominican in the form of Isengrim the wolf, symbolising avarice (Scribner 1994: 119). Further images of Christian sheep and the wolf appeared in German broadsheets during the 1520s.

An edition of William Turner's *The Huntying of the Romyshe Vuolfe, circa* 1555, was published in 1565 with an image of a wolf-bishop biting a lamb as the title woodcut. Malcolm Jones suggested that the inspiration for the woodcut may have come from an image used as the title page of a sermon by the German, Urbanus Rhegius, in 1539 (Jones 2002: 290). Such anti-clerical imagery is less commonly found in England, although there is an early print of a fox as a bishop (Reid 1870: 1). Possibly the rarity of the wolf in the country made it less of an obvious subject for artists. Many of the later prints featuring wolves as clerical figures were either clearly based on continental works or done by foreign artists. Some of the prints will be discussed here, in rough chronological order. These all appear in the *Catalogue of Prints and Drawings* in the British Museum. This is a twelve-volume publication comprising detailed descriptions and biographical information relating to the print holdings at the Department of Prints and Drawings and the Department of Manuscripts at the British Museum. Numbers refer to their number in the 1870 edition edited by George Reid.

## Wolf images in the British Museum's *Catalogue of Prints and Drawings*

10. The *Martyrdom of Reformers* in 1555 shows Catholic priests with wolf heads. The wolf's head metaphor was commonly applied to outlaws. By this time the clergy were seen in some quarters as being separated from reality. The image appears nearly a century later in a secular concept in image 1284.

264. The *Patentee* of 1641 shows a figure with a wolf's head representing parliament stealing. This was probably done by Wenceslaus Hollar, one of several continental engravers working in England.

308. In 1646 Prince Rupert, the grandson of James 1, was depicted with a wolf's head and described as England's Wolfe.

315. *Heraclitus' Dream* of 1642 shows a wolf close to a shepherd with a verse questioning why wild beasts attack a shepherd's flock. It also includes a lion emerging from a wood with a quote from *Jeremiah*, 'A lion of the wood shall slay you.' (*Jeremiah* 5.6) The Devil is on a hillock with the text: 'The Divell is come downe among you.' (*Revelation* 12.12) A leopard is shown threatening a city with another quote from *Jeremiah 5.16*: 'A leopard shall watch your cities.' There is also an owl with a quote from *Isaiah*, 'The Owle and the Stayres shall be there.'(*Isaiah* 13.21) The wolf was not the only animal given negative connotations in satire.

416. In England and Ireland's *Sad Theatre*, 10 January 1645, a wolf is shown trying to raise money at the foot of Archbishop Laud's head. The archbishop was executed on that date.

791. A braver wolf, some five years later, is shown as holding a sword in front of a knife-carrying Pope.

1047. Another image shows a wolf and fox in a sheep's clothing being hung from a tree. Interestingly, the two are shown together, distinct yet connected.

*1146. Converte Angliam circa* 1685 shows a woman, thought to be the Catholic wife of James II, kneeling down before a wolf confessor.

1208. This image of the Catholic wolf appears again in *The Flight of Popery from England* which depicts the French King riding a wolf.

1227. The wolf preaching appears again in 1689. These reflect the anti-catholic sentiments, not helped by what many felt were the pro-catholic policies of James II. This eventually led to his departure to Catholic France and the accession of the protestant William of Orange. It is not clear when wolves first became associated with Catholics but we need to remember that Catholicism in seventeenth century England was regarded as a foreign religion. Catholics were often regarded as outsiders and agents of other European nations. Wolves were also clearly linked with outsiders.

1284. A late-sixteenth/early-seventeenth century print showing a lawyer with a wolf's head. Several groups could be given this connotation of evil which had expanded from its original association with the outlaw.

## Changing image

The image of the wolf underwent certain changes as Christianity grew stronger in a political sense and clearer in an ideological sense. Traditionally wolves, and other wild animals, were portents of doom or instruments of divine punishment employed by God. Subsequently they became viewed as evil in themselves and either servants of the Devil or Satan himself. This process is closely linked with the dissemination of the bestiaries and a greater theological distinction between good and evil forces. Man was no longer afraid of God's vengeance but he was able to despise agents of evil and take action against them. The late middle ages saw an increased tendency within Christian sources to represent evil as an individual force rather than an ideological concept. This was particularly evident in the bestiaries which imposed Christian morality on the amoral animal kingdom.

We do not know how much religion influenced people's attitudes towards wolves in earlier times. There is no record of an increase in hostility towards wolves in England during the Middle Age but there was an increase in witch-hunting fuelled by religious beliefs. Wolves were connected to this by the idea that witches could change themselves into animals, including the wolf. The next chapter will look at the werewolf tradition.

# Chapter four

# The human wolf

A belief in werewolves, and other were-animals, is found in many cultures at many times. Montague Summers gives a detailed list of relevant sources about werewolves in his comprehensive study (Summers 1933) although many more studies have been published since. Most of the texts he cites repeated and modified information in earlier works. Locating the sources of such beliefs reveals the ways later writers altered the ideas to suit their own agendas.

### Werewolves in non-fiction

Early surviving stories and legends about werewolves often treat them sympathetically, as with early tales of real wolves. Herodotus knew a story that every Neurian was able to change himself into a wolf for a few days each year but did not accept it (Herodotus (1996: 4, 105)). Pliny was also sceptical. He described an Arcadian tradition in which someone was said to become a wolf for nine years when, if he had refrained from touching a person, he was changed back (Pliny (1960: 8.81)). Neither Pliny nor Herodotus listed the causes of the transformation but others attributed it to a deity.

Plato knew of a legend associated with the shrine of Zeus (Jupiter) in Arcadia where anyone who ate the flesh of sacrificial victims would become a wolf (Plato (1940: 8.15)). He felt that people who seized absolute power would either be destroyed or become wolves. Greed was a characteristic often associated with the wolf. In his *Metamorphoses*, Ovid describes how Lycaon dared to put human meat before Jupiter and was punished by being turned into a wolf (Ovid (1986: 8.23)).

Most extant sources indicate that in the ancient world individuals were unable to turn themselves into wolves unless they belonged to a specific, often cursed, group. The transformation was usually performed as a punishment by a deity or sorcerer. Werewolves were depicted as victims of magic, not instigators of evil.

### Is lycanthropy a medical condition?

This concept of the werewolf as victim may have a factual origin since some ancient writers regarded lycanthropy as a genuine medical condition. Marcellus Sidetes, *circa* AD 117–61, described an illness which caused men to behave like wolves

(Otten 1986: 10). In the surviving extracts of his poetry he says that cases of lycanthropy were most prevalent at the start of the year, especially February, and that the afflicted went to graveyards.

The idea of lycanthropy as an illness was still around some five centuries after Sidetes when the Roman Paulus Aegineta was writing. He said that people afflicted by lycanthropy imitated wolves and wandered about at night, especially in graveyards (Adams 1854: 359). Their symptoms included pale skin, feeble vision, dry eyes and tongue, no saliva and extreme thirst. Their legs had incurable ulcers as a result of frequent falls. The disease could be cured by bloodletting followed by a three-day diet of milk or whey and purging with *hiera*, which was a herbal preparation. After this a stronger herbal concoction, used for treating snakebites, could be used. If lycanthropy was well established in the patient then liquid could be rubbed on the skin and opium on the nostrils. Aegineta was a serious chronicler of medical and other matters, so it is difficult to see why he would have invented the ailment. He may have been quoting from a fuller version of Sidetes.

Several instances of lycanthropy as a medical condition were cited by Simon Goulart in his *Admirable and Memorable Histories* which was translated into English in 1607 (Goulart 1607: 386–7). In John Webster's *The Duchess of Malfi*, first performed in 1613, a physician diagnoses the disease of lycanthropia in which patients who believed that they were wolves went to graveyards and dug up corpses. A seventeenth century English physician, Robert Bayfield, claimed to have treated a patient for lycanthropy (Bayfield 1633: 51). The symptoms were hollow eyes, scabbed legs and thighs and being very dry and pale.

More recently, modern doctors and writers without medical qualifications have considered the possibility that lycanthropy could be a genuine ailment. Lee Illis, a British neurologist, described a rare condition called congenital porphyria which has symptoms of sensitivity to light, red teeth and a distortion of hands and face (Otten 1986:195–9). Other suggestions include the genetic malfunction, hypertrichosis (which causes the growth of very long hair) and atropine poisoning. The skin condition, erysipelas, was known in France by at least the fourteenth century as *le loup* (the wolf) (Rawcliffe 1997: 138). Despite these attempts to project modern medical knowledge into the past it is difficult to believe that all the werewolves were affected by the same physical illness.

Mental illness offers another possible explanation for incidents of lycanthropy. Goulart refers to men who thought they were wolves, indicating that they were delusional. In a modern case of lycanthropy two psychologists, Harvey Rosenstock and Kenneth Vincent identified the following aspects:

1. Delusion of transformation under stress.
2. Preoccupation with religious phenomenology.
3. An obsessive need to visit graveyards and woods.
4. Aggressive and sexual bestial urges.
5. Physiological indications of acute anxiety.

(Otten 1986: 31–3)

It is not known how many of these patients were influenced by popular images of the werewolf. The modern lycanthropes may consciously imitate the behaviour of their supposed mediaeval predecessors and comparison is difficult. The delusion of transformation under stress may well have applied to earlier cases along with the aggressive and sexual urges. As we have seen, the Romans associated the werewolf with the graveyard, and bereavement can be a cause of stress and mental instability.

Rosenstock and Vincent listed possible causes of lycanthropy as schizophrenia, organic brain syndrome with psychotic depressive reaction, hysterical neurosis of the dissociate type, manic-depressive psychosis and psychomotor epilepsy. None of these ailments was recognised in mediaeval times and the symptoms could have been misinterpreted. Theologians and others were searching for explanations of the strange behaviour.

## Christian explanations of lycanthropy

Early Christian writers debated stories of lycanthropy. Augustine believed that everyone had a phantom which took on various guises as a result of dreams or other hallucinations (Augustine (1984: 18.17)). Another respected authority, Boethius, felt that only the wicked would be transformed (Boethius (1978: 4.4)). This ties in with divine punishment but those who later persecuted werewolves would seek their own retribution.

One example of the werewolf as victim motif is found in the *Topographia Hibernia* of Giraldus Cambrensis (1146–1233). This tells of a werewolf who persuaded a priest to give his lover, also a werewolf, the last rites. Both werewolves were innocent victims of sorcery and the male was credited with the ability to predict the future. He said that England would invade Ireland as a punishment for the sins of the Irish (Cambrensis (1867: 19)). Giraldus wrote after the invasion and is copying the ninth century annalists who portrayed the Vikings spreading divine punishment.

In the twelfth century Gervase of Tilbury stated that werewolves were well-known in England (Leibnitz 1710: 120). He did not provide any examples. Given the apparent rarity of the wolf and the paucity of known werewolf legends in England Gervase may have made a mistake but we can never be certain.

Some extant mediaeval sources confuse werewolf and wolf. *Piers Ploughman* paraphrases the parable in Matthew's gospel about the wolf threatening flocks by substituting werewolf for wolf (Skeat 1867a: 459). The idea of a man-wolf as a man behaving like a wolf is closely related to the idea of a man turning into a wolf.

*The Master of Game* makes a clear distinction between wolves that ate people, referred to as werewolves, and other wolves. This source and Von Kayserberg's sermon indicate that lycanthropy was one of the reasons put forward to explain the abnormal trait of eating people. A comparison can be made with another predator. The concept of a were-tiger might have been invented to explain why some tigers were hostile to humans and others were not (Tylor 1871 (1958: Vol. 1: 280)). No large predators are habitually hostile to humans and none routinely eat humans. Humans living in the same environment as these predators have to account for individual animals which deviate from the normal pattern. This can be done by assuming that those animals are possessed or controlled by another force.

Once eating people was considered an abnormal trait of wolves that could be explained by werewolves, or other supernatural agents, it was incorporated into witchcraft beliefs. In 1605 Verstegan described the werewolves as sorcerers who anointed themselves with an ointment supplied by the Devil. (Verstegan 1605: 264) The idea that people used salves to aid the transformation is commonly found. According to the Victorian writer Sabine Baring-Gould the salves contained deadly nightshade, aconite, hyoscycarmus, belladonna, opium, *Acrous vulgaris sicum* (related to calamus or sweet flag, known to be psychoactive), oil or the fat of a child, and the blood of a bat. Drugs such as belladonna and henbane can cause delusions and would have been available, but there is no evidence that they were used in the documented cases of lycanthropy. A greater number of reported cases would be expected if such drugs were responsible.

**The werewolf in fiction**

One of the first known fictitious stories about werewolves appears in the *Satyricon* of Petronius, an epic novel from the first century AD which has not survived in its entirety. A character called Niceros tells the werewolf tale at a friend's dinner party (Petronius 1959: 59–61). He relates how a man went to visit his girlfriend, taking with him a soldier for company. When they came to a graveyard the soldier stripped, urinated on his clothes and turned into a wolf. The terrified man ran to his girlfriend's house where she reproached him for not having been there to defend flocks against a wolf. The wolf was injured in the attack and the man found the soldier being treated for the same injuries.

The symbolism of this story can be found in many later, purportedly genuine, accounts of werewolves. The graveyard, the discovery of wounds on a human identical to those inflicted on the wolf, the night transformation and the removal of clothes are common motifs. Repeated use of such symbolism strongly suggests that the later stories are invented. Coincidental repetition of fiction must be considered unlikely, especially when the promulgators of the stories were almost certainly familiar with the *Satyricon*.

Few werewolf stories are known to have been disseminated in mediaeval England. One is the Arthurian Romance, *Arthur and Gorlagon* (Milne 1904). In this Arthur is told a tale in which a king (later identified as the narrator) had a sapling capable of changing people into wolves. His treacherous wife used it to transform him but, by mistake, allowed him to keep the understanding of a man. Then she ruled the kingdom with her lover. The king met a female wolf and had cubs, both of which were hanged by the queen. Eventually the werewolf went to a neighbouring province where he alerted the ruler to another treacherous queen. The grateful monarch returned the favour by taking the transformed king home and restoring his form.

In this story the werewolf while in wolf form attacks and kills a number of people, including innocent civilians from his own land. This was despite the retention of his human reasoning and does not sit well with his portrayal as a just ruler. The contradiction indicates that there were originally two stories, one in which the wolf retained human consciousness and one in which it did not.

There is another mention of a werewolf in the collection of Arthurian tales. Thomas Malory refers briefly to Sir Marok who, for a period of seven years, was turned into a wolf by his wife (Malory (1996: 19.11)) Both the Arthurian werewolf stories feature a belief in the treachery of women, a common theme in Christian thought.

Some of the motifs present in the *Arthur and Gorlagon* story are also found in a poem by Marie de France (Burgess and Busby 1986: 68–72). In this tale the werewolf, Bisclaveret, could not return from wolf to human form without his clothes which had been stolen by his wife and her lover. In wolf form he became the servant of the king and was able to obtain his revenge. This is a more coherent version of *Arthur and Gorlagon*. There is no confusion of two separate adulterous wives, and the werewolf does not harm any innocent people.

The story of William and the Werewolf has much in common with the tales told so far. Here again a woman, this time the stepmother, is responsible for the transformation. In the text a werewolf steals a boy in order to save him from treachery (Skeat 1867b). The oldest surviving version dates from the fourteenth century, although it expands on an older French poem. The werewolf adopts the role of servant, tricking people to assist his master. Despite this helpful image a woodcut accompanying a 1522 edition shows the werewolf eating a baby while the king and queen watch, apparently unconcerned. This may be intended to show how the ruling classes regarded their poorer counterparts with contempt.

The first werewolf novel published in England was *Wagner the Wehr-Wolf*, by George Reynolds. This was serialised in *Reynolds Miscellany*, 1846–7. Reynolds was a prolific author who enjoyed much popularity among the working class of his day. Wagner was a German peasant who made a deal with the Devil to receive immortality, on the condition that he became a werewolf every seven years. This is an extension of Pliny's early werewolf story.

Writers of fiction used the werewolf in the emerging genres of science fiction and horror. One of the earliest and best-known examples is *The Werewolf of Paris*, by Guy Endores and first published in 1934. This drew upon the genuine case of Sergeant Bertrand, described by Baring-Gould among others. Bertrand allegedly stole corpses from French graveyards and was court-martialled in 1849. Endores' novel, set in 1870s France, tells how a man named Bertrand commits various murders in the shape of a wolf. For a brief time he finds love but cannot control his urges and is court-martialled after attacking a soldier. He is imprisoned in an asylum where he dies fighting an orderly. There are strong sexual connotations in the novel, indeed the orderly is attempting to rape a female patient when he gets into the fatal fight with Bertrand.

Countless other novels about werewolves have followed. A search using the keyword 'werewolf' in the British Library catalogue in December 2005 revealed five times more entries in the period from 1975 to the present than in the years prior to1975. Clearly there is a demand for lycanthropic fiction, fuelled probably by the number of films about werewolves.

## Hollywood and werewolves

Given that visual sources have a greater impact than written ones it is likely that films about werewolves have been more influential than literature. The werewolf image was made famous by the acting of Lou Chaney Jnr, in *The Wolf Man* (1941). This film tells the story of a young man, Larry Talbot, returning to his father's ancestral home. When trying to save a girl from a werewolf he is bitten and becomes a werewolf himself. Eventually he dies at the hands of his father.

*The Wolf Man* was a seventy-one minute low-budget film with a predictable plot. Yet it succeeded in entering film legend although it was not the first werewolf film. The silent picture *The Werewolf* (1913), later expanded as *The Werewolf of London* (1935), has that particular honour. Films that followed include *The Undying Monster* (1942); *Frankenstein Meets the Wolf Man* (1943); *The Werewolf* (1956); *I Was a Teenage Werewolf* (1957); *Curse of the Werewolf* (1960) which, like *The Werewolf*, was based on *The Werewolf of Paris; The Howling* (1981); *An American Werewolf in London* (1981) and *Brotherhood of the Wolf* (2001), a French film based on the beast of Gevaudan.

Many of these have erotic connotations, far removed from Talbot's romantic interest in a neighbour. In *I was a Teenage Werewolf* the transformation occurs when the werewolf watches an attractive girl doing gymnastics. In *Curse of the Werewolf* a visit to a brothel makes the protagonist mad, just as in *The Werewolf of Paris*, and *The Howling* contains many scenes showing the sex lives of the werewolf colony.

Few of the later werewolf films portray the werewolf as a totally evil being, preferring to focus on the battle for control of the victim's mind. Some are humorous, at least in part, mocking the established image of the werewolf. This has carried through to television; virtually every science fiction series has featured an episode with a werewolf or similar creature. Few portray it as a straightforward monster.

In the British series *Doctor Who* a 1988 story entitled 'The Greatest Show in the Galaxy', written by Stephen Wyatt, saw a pretty woman transformed into a werewolf. She had been captured by a sadistic explorer and later realised that she was able to control the transformation. A story in the *Doctor Who* series broadcast in 2006 portrayed an alien male werewolf attempting to kill Queen Victoria. In between these two tales novels and audio plays in the *Doctor Who* series also featured werewolves.

The arrival of the werewolf in the modern world is perhaps best demonstrated by its appearance in computer games as an adversary along with other familiar foes such as the zombie, skeleton and vampire. The crime library Internet site has a feature on werewolf killers. Typing 'lycanthropy' into Google in March 2006 produced 448,000 hits. A similar search for 'werewolf' on the same date produced eight million matches. The top Web site, werewolf.com, had 4,159 members. This site consisted of discussion boards on various topics, not all of them directly related to werewolves. The second most popular site was a translation of German werewolf tales into English. Some of those tales were incorporated into beliefs about witches and contributed to the persecution of werewolves in Europe.

## Werewolves and witches

By the time of the European witchcraft persecutions in the fifteenth to seventeenth centuries, women were increasingly associated with the Devil. The witch-hunter's bible, the *Malleus Maleficarum*, described women as a necessary evil. Such misogyny had fatal consequences for many females burnt, or in England hanged, as witches although the witch-hunters did not, as is sometimes assumed, exclusively target women.

The persecution of witches by the church was intended as a deterrent. Often the confessions of the guilty usually, but not always, obtained via torture were read immediately before the fires were lit. In this way the watching crowds were taught the elite view of demonology and shown the consequences of a failure to obey. In England, where witches were hung rather than burnt, public executions were not abolished until 1868. They were thought to act as a deterrent.

Witches became the scapegoats for natural disasters. Previously these had been attributed to God's punishment, but increasingly Satan, or his disciples, were viewed as being responsible. The escalation of natural disasters in the middle ages was one of the reasons for this age. The Black Death which swept across Europe during the fourteenth century tested human endurance to the limit. Blaming successive disasters on God would only increase the numbers of heretics and non-believers who were questioning orthodox beliefs that the Church now had the political power to enforce. Blaming Satan was an alternative but he was not visible and the church needed to show the detection and eradication of evil. Thus the execution of witches was a visible sign of the Christian triumph over evil, similar to the ceremonial baptism of the Viking leaders. It reassured as well as deterred.

The witchcraft persecutions introduced the concept of werewolves who wittingly changed themselves, or were changed by Satan, in order to commit evil deeds. This transformed the werewolves from victims into criminals.

The general link between witchcraft and the transformation of humans into beasts had been established in the ancient world. Diodorus tells the story of Lamia, a witch who would transform people into animals and Apulieus also relates transformation stories (Oldfather 1933: 1.10, c.41). Witches were credited with this power and, according to later Christian thought, witches were controlled by the Devil. A direct connection between werewolves and Satan is made in the ecclesiastical laws of Cnut, *circa* 1018, where priests and other spiritual leaders were advised to protect their flocks against the madly audacious werewolf (Thorpe 1840: 160–1).

The werewolf was not generally part of witchcraft beliefs in England, probably because the wolf was rare, or extinct, in the country when the persecutions were most intense. There are a few exceptions. In 1673 an anonymous writer described a vision in which the demon Agrippa said he taught witches to assume the shape of wolves and eat children (Anon. 1673). The idea of witches transforming themselves into other animals was common. In his *Guide to Grand Jurymen*, published in 1627, Richard Bernard listed the following forms that could be assumed by the Devil: man, woman, boy, brown and white dog, foal, spotted bitch, hare, cat, kitten, rat, chicken, owl, toad and crab (Bernard 1627: 106). On the continent lycanthropy was closely linked to the witchcraft trials. This was because the wolf was considered the most dangerous predator and a more suitable shape for the wolf to assume.

### An Examen of Witches

One of the most important French sources on lycanthropy is Henri Boguet's *An Examen of Witches* of 1590, revised in 1602 and 1603. Montague Summers edited an English translation in 1929. Boguet was the chief justice of St Claude from 1596 to 1611. He cites the following historical cases of lycanthropy.

1.  A wolf came among the Roman army that was trying to stop Hannibal from crossing the Alps. It killed some soldiers then escaped.

2.  In 1042 more than fifteen wolves appeared in Constantinople at the same time.

3.  In 1148 a wolf in Geneva killed thirty people.

4.  On 18 July 1603 three wolves were seen in the district of Douvres and Jeurre about thirty minutes after a hailstorm had destroyed all the fruit. They had no tails and ran among goats and cows without touching them, except for one kid which was carried a short way then abandoned, unharmed.

5.  One large wolf preceded the others and Boguet felt that this was Satan. The last story demonstrates how the werewolf and Satan were now closely linked. If the same incident had been described a few centuries earlier it would not have explicitly placed Satan with the werewolves.

Boguet said that three men, Michael Udon, Philient Montot and Gros Pierre had confessed in 1521 that they had changed themselves into wolves and, in that form, had killed and eaten several people. Pictures of this trio were to be found in the church of the Jacobins at Poligny, another deterrent for potential wrong-doers and an example of visual sources being used to influence people. Udon was apparently wounded in wolf-form by a man who followed him and discovered the wound being treated. Boguet tells of a similar case in Apchon, Auvergne, where a gentleman asked a hunter to get a trophy for him. The obliging hunter cut off a wolf's paw which contained a ring belonging to the nobleman's wife. Gervase of Tilbury stated that the severing of a werewolf's paw turns him back into a man and tells of a nobleman in Auvergne who, while in wolf-form, devoured children and old people. His paw was removed by a woodcutter, that familiar protector who crops up frequently in fairy stories of which this tale is surely one, although Gervase implies that he knew the individual. (Leibnitz 1710: 51). In such stories Petronius's fairly harmless fiction was extended with fatal consequences for men such as Michael Udon.

Boguet's work is most interesting when recording his own experiences of dealing with witches who were also werewolves. He describes some cases in detail. Jacques Boquet, Clauda Jamprose, Thievenne Paget and Clauda Jumquillaume confessed that they had killed several children. This was verified by villages from Longchamois and Orciers and by the parents who confirmed that the children had been taken by wolves at that time. Another of the accused Jeanne Perrin said that Clauda Gaillard had turned into a wolf and attacked her in a wood called Fridecombe. She saw Clauda go behind a bush then a wolf emerged without a tail and standing on its hind feet. Afterwards Clauda said that the wolf would not have harmed Jeanne.

Two other alleged werewolves would have been tried with this motley crew but had already been rushed to execution. Pierre Gandillon and his son confessed that they had turned themselves into wolves. The son however insisted that he had never meddled with any children but had, in the company of his aunt Perenette, killed some goats. Boguet said that the peasants killed Perenette as she tried to escape.

Boguet was not the only witch-hunter to recount his experiences. Another was Nicholas Remy whose *Demonolatry* was published in 1593. He blamed witches for all manner of natural disasters and believed that the wolf was the most fitting agent for Satan as it was endowed for depredation better than other animals (Remy 1930 1.23). This is an interesting point as it shows that writers were carefully selecting images likely to have the greatest impact on their audience. Toads and cats may be considered unpleasant by some but they were not generally seen as dangerous to people. They could also be caught and killed more easily than wolves.

Remy was just as credulous as Boguet. He gave three examples of people being wounded in animal form, as wolf, dog and cat respectively, then being identified. One of these was virtually identical to an example given by Boguet and another was told to Remy by the wife of his patron. Whether he believed the story or not he had a reason to publish it.

An intention to demonstrate good triumphing over evil can be detected in the translation and widespread dissemination of a manuscript detailing the trial of a werewolf named Stubbe Peter who was executed in Cologne in December 1589 for a variety of crimes, which included the eating of people and incest. Within six months this illustrated execution broadsheet was available in England and became the most influential source on European werewolves (Anon. 1590). According to the text the Devil gave Peter a girdle that allowed him to change into a wolf. In this shape he supposedly murdered thirteen children and two pregnant women. He would also eat raw lambs and kids. Other offences included incest with his daughter, who had a child by him, and killing his son by a mistress. He was active in these crimes for twenty-five years before confessing, without torture. Stubbe Peter was broken on a wheel which had the likeness of a wolf above it. Bits of wood were placed around the wheel to represent the victims.

The names of the same few werewolves are repeatedly cited in the extant texts, implying that not many others were tried. One study showed that accusations of lycanthropy were fairly common but only a few resulted in prosecutions (Briggs 1996). Despite this some twentieth century writers exaggerated the number of lycanthropy cases, relying on sensationalism rather than facts to sell their books. Caroline Oates made a detailed study of werewolf trials in the Franche-Comté region between 1521 and 1664 (Oates 1993). She noted thirty-nine accusations which reached the courts with thirteen werewolves being executed. Although the trial records and archives have not all survived it is likely that executions would have been recorded in other sources.

## Sceptism

Most English writers living at the time of the witchcraft persecutions were sceptical about lycanthropy. Reginald Scott's *The Discoverie of Witchcraft* is a rare voice of sanity at the time of the witchcraft mania. It inspired King James I to write his *Demonologie* which claimed that witches really did exist. James would later retract his beliefs in spirits and always doubted the reality of werewolves, describing men who pretended to devour women and children (James 1597: 159–60).

Some witch-hunters put forward their own explanations for lycanthropy. The authors of the *Malleus Maleficarum* proposed two. Either Satan created an illusion or he entered real wolves and controlled them (Kramer and Sprenger 1971: 159–60). Boguet followed Augustine in believing that lycanthropy was an illusion since man could not keep his soul in the body of a beast. If the soul was surrendered to the Devil in order to enter the beast then the Devil had to perform a miracle to restore it and only God was capable of miracles (Boguet 1929: 146). Boguet's conclusion from this mass of contradictions was that the Devil committed a crime while the person was asleep then made him or her believe that they were responsible.

The crimes allegedly committed by the werewolves examined by Boguet included the eating of children. Boguet noticed that these werewolves were all scratched on their hands and legs. He also observed that the clothes of the devoured children were found without a single tear, suggesting that they had been removed by human hands. Boguet believed that the witches used knives and swords, dragging the victims over rocks and strangling them. In two cases, Perenette Gandillion and Clauda Gaillard, there is the suggestion that wolf-skins were worn. The idea that werewolves were conventional criminals wearing wolf-skins is worth exploring.

## Were werewolves criminals?

Mary Gerstein argued, mainly from linguistic evidence, that werewolves were identified with outlaws (Gerstein 1974). The outlaw was expelled from normal human society and thus lived like a wolf, without the protection of his peers. Gerstein dealt with Germanic and Norse examples but the connection is explicitly stated in a yearbook of Edward I (Horwood 1866: 237).The Frankish law code *Lex Salica* condemns corpse-violators as *wargs* as does the *Lex Ripuaria*, and the laws

*German woodcut of 1722 depicting a werewolf.*

decreed by Henry I of England (Stone 1994). *Warg* derives from an Indo-European word meaning strangle, which suggests that the use of *warg* in Germanic law codes was a sentence transforming the criminal into a werewolf who should be strangled or hanged. (Gerstein, 1974, 133-34) Hanging was the usual sentence for outlaws.

As harsh punishments awaited people convicted of even minor crimes, the donning of an animal disguise is not implausible. A study of late nineteenth century documents showed that certain groups of African criminals wore animal skins to commit crimes from 1860 onwards (Lindkskog 1954: 25).

If the werewolves were criminals then the accusation of eating people needs to be looked at again. Eating was sometimes used in literature as a metaphor for sex. This raises the possibility that some kind of sexual crime, against children, had been committed. Interestingly some werewolves admitted taking little girls to play with but not eat.

Boguet distinguished werewolves from ordinary wolves by the absence of a tail. Wolves without tails were considered exceptionally unlucky and malign. In folklore the wolf which represented the corn spirit was believed to carry the fertilising power in its tail (Frazer 1993: 448). Boguet's werewolves thus had negative sexual connotations.

There is some circumstantial evidence that the 'eating of children' referred to in trials were not ordinary murders. A werewolf called Garnier, who admitted killing and eating children, was sentenced for lycanthropy and witchcraft, not murder. In fact none of the werewolves were tried for murder and Stubbe Peter was specifically accused of sexual crimes. If children really had been killed then why were the perpetrators undetected for so long? Many were known in the community as recluses, exactly the sort of people who would be suspected of abnormal crimes. If the crimes were sexual then bringing them to justice may have taken a long time.

Crimes against children, especially sexual crimes, were perhaps considered so contrary to accepted social values that the prosecutors had to postulate a special form of insanity or demonic possession for the abuser. In the cases described by Boguet a sexual crime would explain the removal of the clothes, the apparently motiveless murder of children, the absence of confirmed murder victims and the trial of the accused for witchcraft rather than murder. Some modern authorities believe that werewolves, vampires and ghouls were names used in previous times to explain serial killers and predatory sexual killers. Fritz Haarmann, a serial killer in 1920s Hannover, was known as 'the werewolf'. Theodor Lessing's book on his killings borrowed the nickname in its title, *Monsters of Weimar: Haarmann, the Story of a Werewolf*. This was originally published in 1925 and reprinted in 1993 along with Lessing's text on another German serial killer, Peter Kurten. The concept of crimes without an obvious motive is a fairly modern one. Serial killers may have existed in previous times but not until five prostitutes were murdered in London during 1888 were they widely reported.

The idea that werewolves were sexual offenders is intriguing but does not stand up to close scrutiny. Some people were executed during the same period for sexual crimes that were clearly recorded as such. Child-eating is an accusation made against many persecuted groups without factual foundation. Margaret Murray said such accusations are made by a dominant religion against one it wished to suppress (Murray 1970: 122). It is not necessary to agree with her that an alternative religion existed, merely that some were willing to believe that it did and that they then used this belief as a justification to assert their superiority.

Norman Cohn notes that the Jews were accused of murdering children from around the twelfth century onwards (Cohn 1970: 13). Like wolves Jews were outsiders in Christian society. Montague Summers believed that the sacrifices of children by witches and Jews were real (Summers 1973:162). One of the reasons behind his book was a desire to attack the then new religion of spiritualism which he felt to be evil, just as Boguet and the others considered the witches to be evil.

Oates considers that real wolves rather than werewolves were responsible for the deaths of the children and that they would have been properly investigated by the authorities. She noted that many of the werewolves were arrested during wolf hunts. Presumably those hunting an abnormal wolf would be interested in vagrants and hermits acting suspiciously. Oates goes on to comment that the period when werewolves were active was also one which saw a number of wolf attacks on people (Oates 1993: 126). Linnell indicates that 664 people were attacked by wolves in France before 1750, with 477 of those incidents involving non-rabid wolves (Linnell 2002: 120). In his 1508 sermon Geiler Von Kaysersberg postulated lycanthropy as an explanation for man-eating wolves.

Accepting that eating people is an unusual rather than a habitual trait of wolves makes understanding why people believed in werewolves easier. Seeking reasons for the arrival in their locality of wolves preying on humans, they found answers in superstition.

Whatever the reasons for the charges of lycanthropy, the image of the werewolf cemented its place in folklore. This may have been dismissed in England as a purely continental belief but the stories were kept alive by fiction and several secondary studies.

## Secondary studies of the werewolf

The first important non-fiction book on werewolves was written by Sabine Baring-Gould. He makes little distinction between apocryphal tales and those that may possess some truth. The author believed that werewolves were men with an insatiable lust for blood. He failed to prove this hypothesis or to annotate his sources, citing quotations of dubious authenticity. He includes a lengthy section on Gilles de Rais, a fifteenth century French nobleman, executed for the sadistic murder of local children. There may be some truth in the stories he relates but without references it is impossible to analyse the original sources and confirm their veracity. Nonetheless he succeeded in placing lycanthropy in an historical context and many later authors relied on his work.

Montague Summers found similarities between the werewolf and the vampire. These two creatures would frequently be confused by Hollywood and Baring-Gould also discussed connections between them. Summers' books are still being reprinted today although he has attracted a number of critics. Where the information given by Summers can be checked it is rarely verified. As records of fact his books contain little of interest. For students of the macabre they demand reading and helped bring old werewolf stories to a new and more literate audience.

Ebenezer Brewer, writing a dictionary of phrase and fable towards the end of the nineteenth century, described the werewolf as:

> A bogie who roams about, devouring infants, sometimes under the form of a man, sometimes as a wolf followed by dogs, sometimes as a white goat, sometimes as a black goat and occasionally invisible. The skin is bullet proof unless blessed in a chapel dedicated to St Hubert.
>
> (Brewer (1993: 1291–2))
>
> (St Hubert, who died in AD 727, was the Bishop of Maastricht and Liege and is the patron of huntsmen.)

Several supposedly factual books on the topic of werewolves were published during the twentieth century. Few have any scholarly value. More useful for the student of lycanthropy is Charlotte Otten's *A Lycanthropy Reader*, which selects and translates extracts from several primary sources, arranged in various categories. Further research on the topic is often recorded in shorter, more specialised writings. In an obscure article Caroline Stewart suggested that the origin of the belief lay in primitive people wearing the skins of animals for a variety of reasons. These ranged from the pursuit of food to dance, revenge and intimidation (Stewart 1909). There is also a book, based on a lecture, by Robert Eisler which suggests that humanity evolved from peaceful vegetarians to aggressive carnivores and describes the werewolf as a symbol of this transformation (Eisler 1959).

## Contemporary opinions about werewolves

Question fifteen of the survey asked the respondents which country they most associated werewolves with. Expected answers, from the historical evidence of persecutions, were France and Germany. 163 respondents answered this question and the countries attracting five or more votes are listed below.

| Country | Number of Replies |
|---|---|
| Romania | 34 |
| Transylvania | 32 |
| USA | 23 |
| Germany | 13 |
| France | 6 |
| Russia | 6 |
| England | 5 |

If Transylvania is correctly counted with the answers for Romania this makes 66 answers. Transylvania is the home of the vampire and it seems that many respondents confused the Dracula legend with that of the werewolf. Vampires and werewolves have appeared in the same films, notably *Underworld* in 2003 and its sequel in 2006.

The respondents who nominated the USA were perhaps thinking of Hollywood and the various werewolf films. There are some Native American werewolf traditions but these are not widely known. The answers demonstrate that the respondents were more influenced by visual fictitious sources than historical data.

## Recent cases of English werewolves

Occasionally modern werewolves are reported. The most famous English case involves a strange creature seen by several witnesses following the discovery of two Celtic stone-carved heads in Hexham, Northumberland in 1972. The family of the discoverer and their neighbours reported feelings of unease and sightings of a werewolf. The heads were passed to Dr Anne Ross, University of Southampton, for analysis. Unaware of the ghostly experiences she took both heads home. She and members of her family also saw the creature at intervals. When Ross accepted that the heads were the cause of the visitation she passed them on to a collector. The current whereabouts of the heads are unknown but no problems have been reported by either of the two owners known to have possessed them after Dr Ross. A local television company is believed to be making a film about the Hexham heads. Whether this will include a statement from the man who previously owned the house where they were discovered is unknown. He claimed to have made the heads for his children in the 1950s, casting doubt on their longevity.

A British forensic pathologist, Paul Britton, described an interview with a lycanthrope, during which the patient imitated a wolf and howled (Britton 2001: 482–524). This occurred daily at four p.m., a time when the man was normally on a train and able to lock himself in a toilet. Britton had also encountered a man who believed that he changed into a panther and a woman who felt that she could become a cat.

In March 2006 UFO researcher Nick Redfern wrote an article on British werewolves for *Fate* magazine (Redfern 2006). He referred to the case of the Hexham heads and werewolves seen in Flixton, Denbigh, the Hebrides, Abbotsham in Devon and Dartmoor. These cases were not widely publicised and it seems that most peoples' views of werewolves are shaped by films and fiction. This is also true of wolves.

# Chapter five

# The big bad wolf

Over the last two millennia the depiction of wolves in fiction has changed dramatically. In ancient and early Christian stories they were depicted as either an instrument of divine providence or as stupid creatures that could easily be outwitted. Eating people was not one of their characteristics. In later fiction wolves are more commonly portrayed as cunning and evil. How and why did their image change?

## Fables

Wolves often appear in fables and folktales. Most fables that have reached us from the ancient world are attributed to a Greek slave named Aesop, although he is unlikely to have written them all. The earliest extant versions of Aesopic fables were compiled by Babrius, who wrote no later than the end of the second century AD, and Phaedrus, who wrote shortly after AD 31 (Perry 1965). Several mediaeval writers made modifications and additions to these, such as the standard Aesopic text complied by Walter of England (Wright 1997) widely used in the medieval curriculum. English translations of Walter's Latin text followed as usage of the vernacular in literature increased. The most significant is the seventeenth century version by Sir Roger L'Estrange, whose reflections on the tales are often longer than the stories themselves (L'Estrange 1692). In his preface he notes the educational importance of fables and also that Christ used them.

The Aesopic fables are followed by a moral, usually making a general point about life. The collection of animal fables includes such famous tales as the shepherd who cried 'Wolf!' three times, the wolf who spoke ill of the fox to the lion then lost his skin when the fox prescribed it as a cure for the lion's illness, and the wolf who promised to reward a crane or heron for removing a bone from his throat then broke that promise. Perhaps this is the origin of the belief that wolves were treacherous.

In these early fables there is no sense of hostility towards wolves. They are variously depicted as conceited, greedy and arrogant but never malicious or evil. Their most common motivation is the theft of sheep and they usually fail to accomplish this. The narrator does not criticise them for this aim, although it conflicted with human interests. This may imply that ancient farmers and shepherds accepted the loss of livestock to wolves as an occupational hazard. In many later sources, including a few English songs during the thirteenth and fourteenth centuries, the wolf/lamb metaphor appears, as in *The Song of the Times* which repeats the story of the wolf and fox defeating the humble ass before King Lion (Wright 1839: 195–205).

The only Aesopic fable that hints at a belief in wolves eating people is the story of a nursemaid who threatened to throw an unruly child to the wolf. The wolf overheard this and waited in vain. The earliest known version is that of Babrius who adds a description of the wolf's wife scolding him and a comment that women are deceivers. L'Estrange's version features a repeat visit by the wolf to the house in which he heard the nurse praising the child and saying that she would not allow the wolf to get him (L'Estrange 1692: 619). L'Estrange states that the child was motivated more through fear of the wolf than a love of the nurse.

The mediaeval collection known as the *Gesta Romanorum* typifies the development of mediaeval fables and demonstrates the use of pedagogy. One tale relates how a character called Eustacius saw one of his children taken by a wolf and another by a lion (Swan 1877: 194–7). This story may imply that wolves were considered dangerous to children. Chaucer's *The Knight's Tale* contains a curious reference to a wolf devouring a man by the statue of Mars. As Mars was the Roman god of war this may be associating the wolf with battle. It could also be a reworking of the divine providence theme, with the wolf obeying Mars.

**Mediaeval fiction**

When individual wolves appear in mediaeval fiction they are often portrayed as stupid and gullible, similar to their role in Aesop's tales. These characteristics were personified by Isengrim, the principal adversary of Reynard the Fox. Isengrim (whose name means 'one in an iron-mask') first appears in *Ysengrimus* by Nivardus of Ghent in 1150. Caxton's English translation of a later version of Reynard the Fox first appeared in 1481 and enjoyed much popularity. The story, which incorporates and expands upon many earlier tales, tells how Reynard is tried for his crimes and uses a variety of tricks to evade justice. Isengrim is outwitted by the quicker thinking fox. His role is one to be pitied rather than feared while Reynard himself is an immoral hero, being devious, violent and cruel. Such characteristics would sometimes be associated with the wolf, indicating a lack of distinction between canid species.

In 1657 Joshua Poole wrote a text called *The English Parnassus*, which listed the connotations of various words. The wolf was described as 'rapeful, ravening, cursed, Thracian, hungry, greedy, devouring, raping, howling, Appulian mountain, insatiate, bloody, preying, foaming, grinning, night-straggling, gluttonous, furious and savage.' (Poole 1657: 91) Poole described the fox as: 'wily, sly, subtle, thieving, ravenous, greedy, stinking, strong-breathed, bush-tailed, in earth, snarling, cunning, crafty, devouring, pullet-eater.' (Poole 1657: 91) There are many similarities with these two descriptions. In the *Kalendar of Shepherds,* translated into English in 1518 from the French text of 1493, the fox is described as doleful and the wolf as gluttonous (Marchant 1930: 144). As noted in earlier chapters some people still find it difficult to distinguish between canid species.

**Stories for children?**

The next major development in fiction about wolves was the emergence of what are commonly known as fairy stories. Longer than fables these are generally, but not exclusively, aimed at children. Like fables they usually contain a strong moral message and often their characters are rigidly labelled good or bad. Few have an English origin but many have been, and continue to be, popular in England.

*Peter and the Wolf* is a variant on the Aesopic tale of the shepherd who cried wolf, and was made famous by Russian musical renditions. It tells how a bored shepherd's boy twice pretends that the wolf is attacking his charges. The third time there is a real attack and nobody comes to Peter's aid. The wolf is not usually a threat to people in this story, only to their animals. In the original Aesopic version there are several wolves.

Another well-known fairy story is that of *The Wolf and the Three Little Pigs*. The original version is thought to have come to England from native American culture in the early seventeenth century (Pleasants 1994). In this the first pig is female and it is the third that is devoured by the wolf as he is unable to build a brick house. It may be a tale of the conflicting cultural values of the English and the Powhatan. The third pig represents the English, scoffing at the primitive natives and believing that his brick house will be better than the accommodation they can construct with their basic materials. Significantly, this pig fears the wolf more than his siblings. In the most common modern version the first two pigs are consumed while the third outwits the wolf, often because his brick house is better than the others. This sees the triumph of the new values represented by the third pig, and possibly represents the conquest of nature, or of the Powhatan, by the invaders.

In all versions of *The Wolf and the Three Little Pigs,* the wolf is a destroyer. Another version is *The Wolf and the Seven Kids.* In this the mother goat goes out leaving her kids in the house when the wolf comes round. It devours them all, bar the youngest who hides and tell his mother of the tragedy. She gains revenge by scalding the wolf to death. Scalding was also a punishment for the wolf in *Reynard the Fox* and in several other stories. In L'Estrange's version of *The Wolf and the Seven Kids,* the wolf fails to gain entry to the house and the author remarks, 'There are wolves in policy as well as mythology.' (L'Estrange 1692: 28) Clearly he was drawing on the established belief that wolves were deceivers and encouraged his audience to sympathise with the goats.

In all of the above stories the wolf is portrayed as a villain. This may be following the trend established by Isengrim but he was a rather ineffective opponent of Reynard. The wolf, and indeed the werewolf, only became a direct enemy of humanity in Western fiction after Christianity associated the wolf with Satan. These fictitious wolves have deeper motives than sheep stealing, desiring to outwit Reynard or eat Red Riding Hood. The key difference is the crediting of intelligence, albeit limited, to the wolf. In Aesop's tales the wolf is stupid, apart from perhaps the one who disguised himself as a sheep but he was killed anyway. Longer stories discard such one-dimensional characters and decorate them with many more connotations.

*Illustration of the wolf falling into the cooking pot, by L. Leslie Brooke, from* The Golden Goose Book, *(Frederick Warne 1905).*

## Positive images of the wolf in fiction

Not all stories are hostile to wolves. *The Jungle Book,* first published in 1894, describes a pack of friendly wolves adopting the boy Mowgli. Here it is the tiger who is the enemy. Generally in colonial India the tiger was considered more dangerous than the wolf and this is reflected in Kipling's novel. Wolves play an important role in *The Jungle Book,* which is the first modern English work that features a wolf, or wolves, assisting a human.

In the twentieth century a number of short stories and novels featuring wolves appeared. Jack London's *Call of the Wild* and *White Fang* use the individual wolves, or rather hybrids, as central characters and encourage the reader to feel sympathy for them (London 1903; 1906). Both feature violence by men against the canids. However *White Fang* opens with a pack of wolves chasing two travellers and devouring one. Assessing the influence of the story is difficult. Do people remember how White Fang was adopted by the rich man and nearly sacrificed himself to protect that man's family, or how White Fang's mother enticed dogs away from the men so that both dogs and men could be devoured? One of London's themes is that the wilderness belongs to the wolf and that people, especially Westerners, are intruders there. These books are notable for their realistic depiction of events in the natural world. The wolves do not represent or resemble humans. They are animals behaving like animals, without consideration for the actions of humans although both of London's canid heroes develop a bond of affection with individual men.

Question 14 in the survey asked the respondents to name a work of fiction featuring a wolf. This question was answered by 168 people. The works of fiction that attracted five or more answers are listed.

| Work of Fiction | Nominations |
| --- | --- |
| Little Red Riding Hood | 52 |
| White Fang | 19 |
| Jungle Book | 13 |
| Call of the Wild | 10 |
| Company of Wolves | 8 |
| Peter and the Wolf | 7 |
| The Wolves of Willoughby Chase | 6 |
| The Wolf and the Three Little Pigs | 5 |
| The Hound of the Baskervilles | 5 |

Other books retain images of wolves as brutal man-eaters. They are portrayed as the servants of evil in works such as J.R.R. Tolkien's *The Hobbit* and C.S. Lewis's *The Lion, The Witch and the Wardrobe*. Joan Aiken's novel for children, *The Wolves of Willoughby Chase* (first published in 1962), is set in a fictitious nineteenth century where the Channel tunnel has allowed wolves to enter England. In the story two young cousins are threatened by the machinations of a woman wishing to usurp their wealth. The message is that the real wolves are the wicked governess and her sister. Consequently animal wolves become less important, and appear less, as the story progresses. In the earlier chapters their attacks, and indeed presence, appear to indicate forthcoming perils for the heroines. This subtle symbolism strongly reinforces the idea that wolves are dangerous and always willing to devour people.

In the survey Question 14 sought to identify works of fiction that influenced respondents' impressions of wolves; see table above. Red Riding Hood was overwhelmingly the most popular of the nominated works of fiction. Interestingly, five of the respondents picked a novel, Conan Doyle's *The Hound of the Baskervilles,* which does not feature a wolf. They were presumably confused by the hound in the title. Many of these works have been made into films or cartoons, suggesting that visual images were more influential.

What makes Red Riding Hood so memorable? How did this short tale, which first appeared in print in England nearly three hundred years ago, come to exert such an influence over people today?

## Little Red Riding Hood

During the eighteenth century *Little Red Riding Hood* became the first widely disseminated work to portray a specific wolf eating a child. Versions of *Little Red Riding Hood* are found in most European countries and in many other parts of the world. The basic elements are consistently found and can be summarised as follows:

A young girl leaves home to take food to her grandmother. En route she meets a wolf and tells him where she is going. He takes a quicker path, eats the grandmother and disguises himself as her. When the girl arrives she is deceived and eaten. Sometimes she is saved, or freed from the wolf's belly, by a woodcutter, who may also be her father.

The oral version of *Little Red Riding Hood*, in so far as it can now be reconstructed, told the story of a little peasant girl who went to visit her grandmother carrying a basket of bread and butter. A werewolf had eaten Granny, placing her blood in a bottle and her flesh in the bin. When the girl arrives he is dressed as the grandmother and orders her to throw her clothes in the fire. The girl realises that she is about to be eaten and says that she needs to relieve herself. The werewolf allows her to go outside but ties a rope around her legs. She quickly ties this to a tree and scampers off (Zipes 1993: 75).

There may however be an earlier written version by Egbert of Liege in 1023. He tells briefly how a five-year-old girl is taken to a wolf's den where the wolves refused to devour her because of her red tunic (Ziolkowski 1992). Certainly some elements are the same but there are differences, not least the absence of the grandmother and the apparent age of the girl. Red Riding Hood in the oral version could be less than ten but an age of five or below is unlikely. Moreover she is able to outwit the wolf unaided. In Egbert's tale she is saved by the holy status of the cloak. In later versions only a man is able to save her.

The original oral version features a werewolf rather than a wolf. If it is an extension of an earlier tale it supports the idea that lycanthropy was used as an explanation for the abnormal behaviour of wolves that ate people. The original tale is more straightforward than the later stories, explicitly indicating that the man-wolf wanted to have sex with the girl. We return to the metaphor where eating represents sex.

The independence and ingenuity of the first Red Riding Hood is absent in later versions, perhaps reflecting the rigid social structure of succeeding generations. The original oral version reflects a sexual frankness and coarse humour that may have been appreciated more among the peasantry than the bourgeois authors who rewrote the tale. Prominent amongst these was Charles Perrault whose version first appeared in print in France in 1697 and was translated into English in 1729 by Robert Samber.

## Perrault's tale and English variants

Perrault's Red Riding Hood was naïve rather than quick-witted. She does not escape from the wolf and the story focuses on her disobedience. She is guilty of speaking to the wolf and accordingly is punished by being eaten. Perrault is implying that girls should obey their parents and learn to curb disobedient impulses. His moral describes wolves that ogle and leer and leaves us in no doubt that he is referring to a man (Perrault 1725: 6–8). The wolf may also represent a divine punishment for the girl's curiosity. Modern parents warn their children not to talk to strangers; three centuries ago Charles Perrault was spelling out the consequences for those who failed to heed this warning.

A slightly altered version of Perrault's tale appears in a book for English children in 1799 (Anon. 1799: 28–32). The book begins with simple exercises aimed at teaching children the alphabet, vowels and consonants. It then relates the story of Cinderella, followed by Red Riding Hood. Again there is no reprieve for the girl. Presumably this was not intended for children to read themselves, since a child who is only just learning letters would be unable to cope with a whole story. Rather it must have been designed for adults to read aloud. No illustrations accompany the text so the influence would depend on the way in which it was delivered orally by the parent or guardian. This edition reveals the popularity of Red Riding Hood as it was selected for inclusion ahead of other tales.

In another version of the story printed in London in 1808 the girl is good, merely careless in talking to strangers (Anon. 1808). Here the tale is used to educate and instruct. Again the girl is killed, a harsh warning, but this was an era when parents would keep copies of *The Newgate Calendar*, with its lurid accounts of various English criminals, to discipline and deter their children. John Marshall's edition of 1823 also sticks to Perrault's tale. In the illustrations here the wolf is depicted upright and dressed as a man, although he has no shoes.

## The Brothers Grimm

After Perrault the most popular version of the Red Riding Hood story is that of the Brothers Grimm, first published in England in 1823. The most significant difference is the alteration of the ending, to show the woodcutter saving the girl. This permits the Christian idea of redemption and also shows that evil can be defeated. Jack Zipes claimed that the Grimms' collection was the second most widely-read book in Europe after the Bible (Zipes 1993: 36). Certainly it was influential but not the only version of Red Riding Hood available in England.

In the edition of *Red Riding Hood* published by William Weeks in 1834 the wolf is depicted back on all fours and devoid of clothes. Again this follows Perrault's tale but adds a description of the wolf being killed by angry villagers. It had become expedient to depict the wolf as evil and to show that evil being punished.

In the *Blue Beard Picture Book* of 1875 the wolf is back dressed as a man, although the shawl he wears when accosting Red Riding Hood in the woods could be that of an old woman. He is shot by a sportsman before consuming the girl (Crane 1875). In an 1893 edition Perrault's ending was restored (Adams 1893). This text had black and white illustrations. The influence of drawings and stories on impressionable children should never be underestimated.

*Illustration of Red Riding Hood and the wolf by Gustave Dore, 1867.*

Red Riding Hood was intended, as we can see from the books listed above, to be read aloud to young children. The parent or storyteller could easily scare the child with their delivery of the eating scenes. Both Angela Carter and Cristina Bacchilega remembered being told the story as children (Bacchilega 1997: x–xi, 69–70). In the nineteenth century children in England would not have access to other information about the wolf. Red Riding Hood must have played a part in encouraging them to fear wolves.

Neil Gaiman's *Wolves in the Walls*, first published in 2003, was inspired by the author's daughter having nightmares about wolves in the walls. This story about the nightmare coming true is aimed at children nine years or older. Red Riding Hood is now aimed at a younger group but some see adult connotations in the story.

**Interpretations and sexual connotations**

If the wolf in the Red Riding Hood story is symbolic of a man then it becomes easier to view the story as a parable of rape. By this interpretation frightening males linger in the woods to prey on hapless females. The girls are better advised to stick to the path and not stray into forbidden territory. This makes the victims indirectly responsible for the crime. Red Riding Hood ignored the warning of her mother and abandoned the single direct route for a more pleasurable one. The implication is that she was to blame for consciously straying from the straight path towards stability and convention or for allowing herself to be tempted. Such an interpretation would depend on the age of the girl. Most versions since the seventeenth century place her back at the lower scale of the age range. This succeeds in making the character of the wolf more menacing and evil because children are commonly perceived as innocent.

Red Riding Hood's character may also have been intended to be innocent and the tale might reflect the loss of that innocence by describing a first sexual encounter. In these circumstances one is nervous and unsure precisely what to expect. The experience has been described as pleasurable and desirable but there remains a sense of danger and experimentation. Are these the conditions parodied by the girl's comments on the hirsute body of her companion? The ritual undressing and the chosen vocabulary support this idea as do many of the engravings which accompany the early texts. Some teenagers must have been tempted to sample the forbidden world of intimacy or have been enticed into it by older, predatory males.

There is much to commend the theory that Red Riding Hood is a story about sex. The sexual overtones, the wolf's invitation for the girl to join him in bed, the possible menstrual connotations of the red cap and ultimately the act of consumption all support this. The tale might be seen as a parable to discourage adultery or promiscuity or merely discourse with strangers. The instilling of fear into the minds of the readers or listeners might be the intention. In this sense the story functions as a deterrent.

Before the widespread availability, acceptance and promotion of contraceptives a promiscuous girl was likely to become pregnant and could be ostracised by society. There would be a social impact on their families as well. Men were interested in restricting, or controlling, the sexual freedom of women. In Perrault's tale and the early English adaptations it was thus necessary for the girl's punishment to be harsh and final. The Grimms did not see this necessity but there are, perhaps, unpleasant connotations in their version. Zipes pointed out that the collection of tales collected by the Grimms contains twenty-five in which the main focus is on children being abused. This does not include stories where children were kidnapped, abandoned or where the parents made pacts with the Devil to surrender them (Zipes 1988: 120). In the light of this the idea that werewolves were sex offenders does not seem outlandish.

Perrault cast Red Riding Hood as a victim. Rape was the punishment that awaited all girls who strayed from the right path. Several English books and stories published in the nineteenth century contained a moral message and warned against the pursuit of illegal or illicit entertainment. Thomas Hardy's *Tess of the D'Urbervilles* and George Eliot's *Adam Bede* are examples. In both of these texts and in *Red Riding Hood* the vulnerable and naïve females were punished for their perceived crimes.

Perrault had to alter the conclusion in which the girl escaped, in order to show that the forces of evil were stronger than a mere peasant girl. Her death symbolised not only the loss of innocence but also of childhood and conventional life, through her own naivety. She forgot, or ignored parental warnings and went to explore an environment which she was ill-prepared for. The erosion of innocence by experience should have been delayed until maturity came. The Grimms were content to describe the girl's experience as a warning.

Many of the illustrations to the tale in English books show Red Riding Hood smiling in bed. She had become a seductress, a willing participant in the liaison with the wolf. Attitudes towards sex had changed in Christian ideology. Originally the male desire had been considered sinful but gradually it became seen as excusable due to the temptations presented by women.

Zipes argued that the Red Riding Hood tale was used in propaganda directed against women and that it reinforced images of women as tempters, agents of the devil, witches and generally inferior to men. The emerging European middle classes were interested in preventing the emancipation of women. This is comparable with the way that wolves were portrayed as evil in Christian ideology and as eaters of people by those with economic reasons for desiring their extinction.

The use of wolves as metaphors for divine punishment means the wolf in *Little Red Riding Hood* might also be seen as an agent of divine retribution punishing the girl for failure to go to church, for disobeying her parents, or perhaps just for being naive.

Perrault stresses the importance of maintaining social order by suggesting that people who behave in an inappropriate way are punished. His Red Riding Hood could not escape as she did in the peasant's tale. When his conclusion was revised by the Grimms and others the girl was still punished but saved by a man. This portrayal of men as seducers or protectors emphasises that the fate of the girl depended on them and, unlike in the original version, not on her own initiative.

Zipes pointed out that fairy tales lost their ideology as they were transmitted through literary texts (Zipes 1988: 12). His thesis is that Perrault transformed the oral tale which showed the girl using her initiative into one in which she is the victim. There are similarities here with the way in which the role of the wolf, and indeed werewolf, changed within fiction over a period of time.

The wolf appears as the enemy because children were familiar with men in the guise of fathers, brothers, uncles and neighbours. They would not automatically fear encountering them in the woods. The wolf was little-known and portrayed already as an eater of children. It was sent to teach a lesson, harking back to the notion of divine punishment. The girl could not save herself.

### Red Riding Hood in the twentieth century

Various modern versions are more sympathetic towards the wolf. This may be because the roles of women have changed within society and in many cases women are rewriting the tales. Versions in which the girl defeats the wolf are uncommon before the Second World War. Following this society changed, granting more freedom to women, allowing the development of a more critical media, and producing a generation who were aware of environmental issues. The idea of protecting wolves from humans was unthinkable in previous times.

The most significant modern version of Red Riding Hood is Angela Carter's 'Company of Wolves', originally published in 1979. The sexual connotations were explicitly stated here and the independence of the girl fully restored. It begins by describing several werewolf myths and suggests that Red Riding Hood was a sexual predator. Carter's heroine promises the wolf a kiss if he reaches the grandmother's house before her. Once there she willingly accedes to his sexual demands and manages to tame him. This was made into a film in 1984, written by Carter and Neil Jordan.

Carter took old ideas and made them relevant to a fresh audience. Some of her peasant characters believe implicitly in wolves eating people, although she is subtly mocking that and other beliefs. For example, the character of the lycanthropic duke who looks after the wolf-girl Alice appears to be based on a character in a seventeenth-century play, *The Duchess of Malfi*. In 'Wolf Alice' Carter blends the separate notions of a child raised by a wolf and of a man transformed into a wolf (Carter 1995: 221–30).

Catherine Storr wrote three short story collections of children, portraying a wolf that tried to eat a child. Her tales of *Clever Polly and the Stupid Wolf* describe the wolf's attempts to catch and eat the seven-year old Polly (Storr 1982: 1985; 1990). In the main these stories are told from the wolf's viewpoint. His continued failure and stupidity do not make him a wholly unsympathetic character however. His plans are often derived from fairy stories and fables such as *Little Red Riding Hood, Goldilocks and the Three Bears* and *Hansel and Gretel*. There is more than a suggestion that he thinks chasing the little girl is how a wolf should behave rather than such pursuit being part of his nature.

Like Carter, Storr mingles fantasy with reality. As is common in fairy stories, animals interact with each other and with humans, ignoring usual restrictions of language and behaviour. Only in Storr's final tale, *Kind Polly and the Wolf in Danger,* do the other human characters identify the wolf as unusual (Storr 1990: 89–102). Prior to that he mingles with them unnoticed, conducts conversations and is able to perform mundane tasks such as shopping.

Roald Dahl also draws on traditional fairy stories. His *Revolting Rhymes* includes a version of 'The Three Little Pigs' in which the third pig calls on Red Riding Hood for help. She draws a pistol from her knickers and shoots the wolf but then turns the pig into a travelling case. Dahl's tale has come full-circle, restoring the independent resourceful girl. In the late twentieth century there was no need to portray the wolf as evil in the Red Riding Hood story. Warning children against talking to strangers could be done by letting them see media reports of murders.

While the image of the wolf in Red Riding Hood was being used to frighten Victorian and Edwardian children, stories about a very different wolf were being circulated in England. They alleged that wolves were raising children in their dens. Stories of wolf children are so numerous as to deserve a chapter of their own.

# Chapter six

# The mother wolf

Stories of wolves, and other animals, raising children date back to ancient times. In the classical world a child suckled by an animal would often become a hero. Herodotus remarked that a rumour concerning Cyrus being suckled by a bitch was spread by Cyrus's parents in order to gain him this prestige (Herotodus 1996: 1.122). Generally an animal foster parent was believed to pass on its characteristics to the child. This was considered beneficial as it made the recipient superior to other humans.

One of the best-known tales is that of Romulus and Remus who were allegedly suckled and reared by a she-wolf after being abandoned on the banks of the river Tiber. They went on to found the city of Rome. There is no evidence that this actually happened or even that the boys existed. As the Latin word *lupus* means both prostitute and she-wolf there may not have been any wolves in the original story. Romulus and Remus were well-known in England, being depicted on the left side of the Franks casket which was probably made in Northumbria, *circa* AD 650. This image shows the she-wolf suckling the boys whilst her mate licks their toes. The cover to a late seventeenth century English history of Rome shows the wolf between the boys (Florus 1669).

A distinction must be made between children supposedly suckled by animals and those supposedly raised by them. Surprisingly few cases of animals raising children also contain stories of suckling. E. McCarthy identified forty cases of animals raising children in Greco-Roman culture and nine of them raising gods (McCarthy 1924: 27). Only six of the children were girls and he was unable to find similar examples involving girls in other cultures. If animals were actually raising children then there should be no disparity between the sexes, especially as girls were perhaps more likely than boys to be abandoned due to the perceived greater value of a male child.

One of the more interesting early stories is that of a goat boy, told by Procopius who wrote in the sixth century AD (Procopius (1914: Vol. 3. VI. XVII, 1–11)). The boy, later named Aegisthus, was suckled by a nanny goat which protected him like a human mother. Presumably this and most of the classical accounts were known to the educated in mediaeval England and Europe.

Whether stories of animals raising children are true or not, people, including children, were living wild in many areas and continue to do so. In Europe the

*Etruscan bronze statue of a she-wolf,* circa *500–480 BC. The boys were added in the fifteenth century.*

presence of hermits, outlaws, and criminals added some credence to legends. Further the existence of the exposure motif in stories such as *Hansel and Gretel* suggests that poor parents were tempted to dispose of unwanted offspring by leaving them in the wilderness. This practice may continue in some countries and stories of modern wild children appear in countries such as Romania. Sightings of wild children may also have contributed to werewolf myths.

**Green and other wild children**

Two mediaeval English chroniclers record a story of two wild children found in a wolf pit at the village of Woolpit near Suffolk during the reign of King Stephen, possibly in 1173 (William of Newburgh (1856: 27); Ralph of Coggeshall (1875: 118–20)). The children, who were apparently coloured green, were taken to the home of Sir William de Caine at Wilkes but their final fate is unconfirmed. Despite the sparse accounts in the chronicles these children have appeared in later literature with several books, factual and fiction, exploring their origins. The children, and a wolf which does not appear in the story, can be seen on the village sign.

A wild boy, later named Victor, was found in Aveyron at the start of the nineteenth century. He had been roaming wild for years and opinion was divided as to whether he was an imbecile or a normal child traumatised by the experience. However he was not linked to animals, being able to fend for himself and surviving for some time prior to his capture. There was also a boy called Peter found in Hamlin in 1724 but later brought to England, on instructions from King George I, where he died in 1785. His tomb is outside the church of St Mary's in Northchurch, Hertford. Inside there is a brass tablet containing a picture of Peter as an old man and a brief history. The inscription reads:

> To the memory of Peter, known as the Wild Boy,
> having been found wild in the forest of Hertswold near
> Hanover in the year 1725. He then appeared to be
> about 12 years old. In the following year he was
> brought to England by the order of the late Queen
> Caroline, and the ablest masters were provided for him.

But proving himself incapable of speaking, or of
receiving any instruction, a comfortable provision was
made for him at a farm in this parish, where he
continued to the end of his inoffensive life. He died on
the 22nd of February, 1785, supposed to be aged 72.

Children could easily be abandoned or lost in the thick forests and woods that once covered so much of Europe. One case in the nineteenth century involved a six-year old girl who followed a wolf into the woods and was discovered some six weeks later (Davies 1875: 257). A more recent case involved a Romanian boy living wild with dogs for some time but at least one British newspaper (*Daily Telegraph* 14 April 2004) referred to him as a wolf boy.

## Characteristics of wild children

A naturalist who examined Victor of Aveyron identified several characteristics of wild children. These included dark skin, scars, large thumbs, frightened expressions, the eating of raw meat (Victor did not eat any meat at all at first), a hatred of children, an ability to climb trees, and to walk on all fours (Lane 1971: 47).

Possibly the children had some kind of psychiatric illness or learning difficulties such as dyspraxia. Mentally-deficient children would be shunned in mediaeval society as they are often are today. Some of these wild children would have come into contact with wolves and garbled accounts of the encounters could lead to rumours about wolves raising children or eating them. Bruno Bettelheim proposed three reasons why such children were confused with wolves. They did not talk, shunned human company and made ferocious attacks (Bettelheim 1967: 357–8). Perhaps some people believed that the children had been wolves in a former life.

## Wolf children in India

Few European stories of wild children feature wolves and for those that do there is no extant evidence. Some cannot even be dated and none appear to have been widely known in England. However there are some stories of wolves raising children in India during the nineteenth and twentieth centuries. Our knowledge of them comes mainly from the accounts of British officials.

There are a relatively small number of second-hand reports which were brought to the attention of British military officers in India during the mid- to late-nineteenth century. Written records survive in the form of memoirs and literature left by the officers. In most cases they were not keen on disseminating the material. This may be because they did not accept it as fact or because they had no real interest. There were probably many more wolf-children noted in local folklore.

Colonel William Sleeman (1809–56) was the first European to publish details of Indian wolf children. He obtained information from oral sources and from the private diary of another British official which has not survived. Sleeman's fifteen page pamphlet entitled *An Account of Wolves Nurturing Children in their Dens* first appeared in 1852 and the information was also included in his book, *A Journey through the Kingdom of the Oude* (Sleeman 1971). He listed the following cases of wolf children found in the Oude district.

1. Two men saw three wolves with a boy on the banks of the river Gumptji. They took him to Lucknow where wolves apparently visited him during the night.

2. A boy aged nine or ten was found by a trooper in a wolf's den near Chandour, ten miles from Sultanpoor in 1847 or 1848. He was scared of people and ate like a dog. The Rajah of Hansunpoor sent him to Captain Nicholetts whose letters are the main source of Sleeman's knowledge. The boy died in August 1850. He was claimed by his original parents but they declared him stupid and abandoned him. Sleeman states that he never spoke until he said 'It aches', and asked for water which he quaffed then died. These would be unusual first words. The only evidence that the boy was found in the wolf's den is that of the trooper, reported at least first hand. This boy may have been mute but he was probably not an authentic wolf child.

3. A boy aged three was snatched by a wolf at Chupra, twenty miles east of Sultanpoor in March 1843. In February 1849 two men found the boy with some wolf cubs and took him to Kolee bazaar where he was identified by his mother on account of a birthmark on his thigh, a scald on his left knee and teeth marks on his loins. He preferred raw meat to other food and was not affectionate. All this was supposedly confirmed by neighbours and villagers. In November 1850 Captain Nicholetts ordered both boy and mother to be sent to Sleeman but the boy ran away. At first glance this story appears more believable than its predecessor. The boy was at an age when he could conceivably have been carried away by a wolf. However as Sleeman was unable to confirm what the villagers told Nicholetts and Nicholetts did not leave a written record, this case must also be dismissed.

4. The Rajah of Hansunpoor said that in 1843 a twelve-year old boy came to Hansunpoor, having been brought up by wolves. He could walk erect but was unable to speak. His parents recognised him. Again there were no eyewitnesses.

5. A shepherd from Ghutkoree, twelve miles from Sultanpoor, saw a boy with a wolf. The child was captured and taken to Colonel Gray but a few days later ran off. There is no evidence whatsoever to support this story.

6. According to Zulhikar Khan, a landowner in Bankipur, some eight or nine years earlier than the date of interview in 1849 a trooper rescued an eight- or nine-year-old boy from wolves. The boy was mute but understood sign language. He was looked after by a cultivator for three months then claimed by a shepherd as his son. He had no body hair. This tale was confirmed by the village people. Presumably that confirmation was confined to information given to them by the trooper.

7. In 1842 or 1843 another trooper and his companion captured a boy, aged around ten. Firstly he was looked after by the Rajah then by a comedian who both let him go. He was shot with an arrow by a shopkeeper and subsequently cared for by Janoo, a servant of Sanaoolah. Four months later he began to understand signs. On several nights he played with wolves, of which there were never more than four. Eventually he ran away. Two months later a woman from Chureya Kotra came to the Rajah and

claimed him as her son, identifying him by describing two marks, one on his chest and another on his forehead. Sanaoolah, Janoo and other servants confirmed the story although the Rajah could not recall seeing the mother, when he wrote to Sleeman on 28 January 1851. This story is more detailed than the others and differs from them in two important respects. Firstly the boy was examined over a period of time. Secondly the identification made by the mother came after the boy had escaped, and she had to travel a long way to make the claim. This would suggest a genuine motive.

## Common factors in Sleeman's stories

There are three common factors in the stories reported by Sleeman. The wolf children were all male, were usually discovered by one or two people who claimed to have seen them in the company of wolves and were claimed by parents. Bearing in mind that several years had elapsed in each case since the supposed disappearance one must ask how reliable the identifications were. It should also be noted that many poor families in India relied on healthy male offspring to run businesses and perform domestic duties. Parents without male children may have made false claims on orphans, perhaps without realising the extent of their abnormal behaviour.

Sleeman did not see any of the boys himself and maybe he was merely recounting garbled recollections of idiot children found in the jungle. Indeed he was sceptical, noting that none of the stories had been authenticated. He did speak to a man who had supposedly been rescued from a wolf's den by a hermit but concluded that there was no evidence. He believed that a child raised by wolves could never attain human intellect and further considered that children in a wolf's environment would have difficulty surviving for long periods.

## Accounts from other officials

Sleeman was not the only person to comment on wolf children in the nineteenth century. In a paper read in 1880 Jivanji Jamsedji claimed to have seen a man known as 'wolf-boy' at Agra in March 1878 (Jamsedji 1880). He also quoted from Reverend Lewis's *History of Secundra Orphanage* where three other wolf children had supposedly been taken. One boy was sent to Secundra by the magistrate of Bulandahar with a claim that the magistrate had smoked him out of the den. He could not speak but learnt to walk erect and it was supposed that the she-wolf had claimed him as a substitute for the cubs. Again the account of the discovery is suspect.

According to Jamsedji two other boys were taken to Secundra on 5 March 1872 when a man called Erhardt was Superintendent. The boys were found by locals who were hunting wolves. One died shortly after his arrival but the other stayed there for at least six years.

In 1873 Valentine Ball read a paper on wolf children to the Asiatic Society of Bengal (Ball 1880:128–30). In it he referred to a letter from Erhardt concerning the two boys. One boy was brought to the orphanage on 5 March 1872 from Mynpuri. The other was fourteen years old and had been at the orphanage for six years. Erhardt also referred to a mad fellow at Lucknow asylum whom Ball believed to be the man captured on the banks of the River Gumpti. Not all the members shared Ball's enthusiasm and the committee agreed to write to the orphanage and the asylum for further information. From the silence in the records thereafter apparently no satisfactory response was received.

Ball claimed that one of the boys at Secundra was taken into a magistrate's court with the dead wolves (Ball 1880: 454). Even if this was true, and the court records were extant, it still would not prove that the boy was found with the wolves. Erhardt said that a man dug out of a wolf's den by a European doctor was at Lucknow madhouse.

According to the Assistant Commissioner of Sultanpoor in 1860–1, Mr H.G. Ross, the police brought in a boy said to have been taken from a wolf's den (*The Field* 1895: 786). The boy was then four years old and grew up to join the police force. However Ross did not recount his experience until over thirty years later.

Another wolf boy in the province of Oude was described by *The Times* on 20 October 1873. This story was apparently circulating in several Indian papers although *The Times* specifically credits *Allen's Indian Mail*. The boy, aged twelve or thirteen, had apparently been captured two or three years earlier and interviewed shortly afterwards. He was apparently not dissimilar from other boys of his age and could recite his experiences, describing how the wolf pack used to hunt. The report mentions other stories of wolf children and concludes that this case is superior. Unfortunately this conclusion cannot be supported now. Firstly there are no details of the precise place or dates for either the capture or the interview. Secondly ten years had passed between the interview and the publication of the story.

In a report in *Lippincott's Magazine*, in 1895 a Mr Greigh of the 93$^{rd}$ Sutherland Highlanders declared that, when his regiment was marching toward Bareilly in 1858 after the taking of Lucknow, he saw at Sahjejan an individual said to have been raised by wolves (*Lippincott's Magazine* 1898: 121). The same boy was also seen by a Mr H.D. Wilcox of the Bengal Civil Service (*The Field* 1896: 619). Neither witness observed the boy in the company of wolves nor had any firm evidence as to the nature of his upbringing.

During their investigations into a later wolf child incident William Ogburn and Nirmal Bose were informed by a Mr Sarat Dutt of a wolf child, aged about 15, in 1899. He had been captured by forest workers in the United Provinces near Nepal. A Mr and Mrs Seth identified him as their child, abducted six years earlier at the age of two. What they made of the age difference is unclear (Ogburn and Bose 1959: 165–6). This story is from a different area than most of its predecessors and therefore implies that similar tales were known across India. However, as it was still being recounted some sixty years or so afterwards, similar stories were probably uncommon.

A twelve-year old wolf boy was found when Mark Thornhill was magistrate of Mutt (Thornhill 1899: 279). Thornhill was sceptical, believing that it was the child of a vagrant and that there was no evidence to support stories of wolf-children.

Mervyn Smith described the capture of a wolf-boy aged around ten who he thought had been assisting a man-eating wolf (Smith 1904: 96). His book includes a photo of the boy, named Seaall, taken ten days after his capture. Later the boy was sent via Bjopal with Lieutenant Cumberledge to a missionary. Smith believed that this was the original Mowgli. However he did not provide firm evidence to connect the boy with the wolf.

William Ireland made some useful comments on the subject of wolf-children although he drew most of his information from Sleeman. He said that the boy in a wolf's den near Chandow died in August 1850 (Ireland 1900: 429–32). He then cites various letters referring to wolves suckling children, specifically to two boys in 1871, and also to wolves eating people.

*The Observer* on the 19 November 1916 published five letters relating to wolf children. The first from Arthur B. Urmston referred to his father Colonel H. Brabazon Urmston who was commissioner of the Rawalpindi Division between 1860 and 1874 and saw a wolf boy on an unspecified date. The letter then quotes at length from the Christian Missionary Society's Secundra orphanage report for 1872 written by Mrs Erhardt. This refers to two wolf boys discovered in that year and taken to the orphanage. One was an eight-year old from Mynpoorie. He was deaf and dumb, enjoyed raw meat and did not walk unless led. He liked living in dark places and often tore up his clothes. One boy remained alive, but was deaf and dumb. The other died. This information does not exactly tally with that provided by Jamsedji or Ball.

The writer of the second letter published in *The Observer* claimed to have seen a thirty-four-year-old former wolf boy in an asylum in Bengal. The third letter from J.A. Hither, enclosed a photograph of a wolf-boy Sanichar which the editor thought was not good enough to print. This boy was captured in fields in Agra and taken to an orphanage at Silkandar near Agra. He never learnt to speak.

The fourth letter from M. Novis says that a twenty-year old wolf child was seen in Lucknow in 1892. The boy did not speak but seemed healthy.

The fifth letter from M.H. James refers to a mission printed text sent to him by an army chaplain. This contained an account and picture of a wolf boy. He was about twenty-five, deaf and dumb. Unfortunately James had not retained the text.

## Wolf girls found in Midnapore

All these cases are interesting but none of them contain any real evidence that children were raised by wolves. There is however an account which describes two girls being discovered in a wolf's den and narrates their subsequent growth and development. This is recorded in the diary of the Reverend Joseph Singh who, in the company of other witnesses, allegedly rescued the girls in 1920. The diary was not published until 1942, being rejected on a number of occasions because of the poor quality of the, now lost, manuscript and doubts over its reliability (Singh and Zingg 1966). Such doubts persist as Singh was credited with a different account of the discovery. Nevertheless he is the only alleged eye-witness of the discovery of a wolf-child who has left a detailed contemporary, or near-contemporary, record.

Singh was in charge of an orphanage at Midnapore when in 1920 a man named Chunarem alerted him to stories of mysterious beings in the area of Godamuri. Singh claimed to trace them to a wolf's den under a large termite mound. This appears to be the only account of a wolf's den under a termite mound and if Singh was inventing the story one would expect more convention. According to his diary Singh returned to the termite mound in the company of several Indian hunters and two Europeans, named as Mr P. Rose and Henry Richards. They began to dig out the den. Two male wolves fled but a female resisted and was killed. Inside were found two human girls and two wolf cubs. One of the girls was aged five or six and the other about three. Immediately this differs from other stories which all featured single boys. Also the area is different, not being in Oude. The presence of two unrelated girls in the den suggests that the circumstances leading to their involvement with the wolf pack were not unique. Singh named them Kamala, meaning 'lotus', and Amala, meaning 'bright yellow flower'.

At this stage there was no publicity about the discovery. Full details were only provided after the deaths of the girls. Dr S.P. Sarbadhicari was summoned to treat Amala's final illness on 11 September 1921. She died ten days later and was buried in St John's churchyard under a banyan tree. Neither girl had received medical treatment at the time of the rescue.

## Kamala's life

Kamala survived and lived at the orphanage. She ate raw meat, including carcasses. At first she could not touch salt. She had a high jawbone and could not stand without assistance. Her eyes glared and she was unable to tolerate the sun. She took to a hyena cub, which returned her affection, and ate from the same plate as dogs. Gradually the situation changed. Kamala became frightened of dogs which were now barking at her, and she started to use the toilet. By 1926 she knew around thirty words, mostly the names for utensils and household goods. Any hopes that this progress would continue and eventually allow her to lead a normal life were extinguished by her death on 13 November 1927.

The deaths of both girls are apparently recorded in the register of burials at St John's church. Dr Sarbadhicari supposedly said that they died of kidney failure caused by an inability to get used to a normal diet. This suggests that they were malnourished prior to the discovery although this was common for many Indian families and Singh's wife would later die of starvation.

## Was the diary genuine?

There is much detail in the diary, much of it unnecessary in a forgery. However the record of the girls' behaviour may be genuine with the details of their discovery

*Kamala in the orphanage grounds. Photo taken by Rev Singh.*

being false. Why should Singh falsify the details? One possibility is that he desired publicity to help ease the financial problems facing the orphanage. In a diocesan report of 1921 he mentions severe financial pressure (MacLean 1977: 141). Yet if he wanted to tempt philanthropic hearts he could have done so by saying that the girls came from prostitutes. There is no evidence that he sought to profit from the girls. On the contrary there is evidence that he tried to avoid publicity in 1920 and he certainly did not desire it in 1921. In the diary he bemoans the curiosity of sightseers drawn to the orphanage after Sarbadhicari had published details of Amala's origins. The story was not reported in the West until 22 October 1926 when the *Westminster Gazette* published an article.

Singh is known to have taken children of prostitutes and pagan tribes back to the orphanage. A story supposedly appeared in *The Calcutta Statesman* on 16 November 1926 to the effect that the wolf girls came from these unfortunates. According to this account Singh was journeying through Mayurbhanji when a poor cultivator of the Jodha tribe took him to his hut and showed him the children. Later Singh went back and was told that the villagers had removed the girls from the wolf's den, which he was shown.

In March and April 1940 Singh sent letters in which he claimed to have told the original story to Bishop Pakenham Walsh in October 1926. In the London archives of the Church Missionary Society Charles MacLean came across a brief mention of the wolf children in the Calcutta diocesan record. There Singh said that the two girls were rescued by villagers and given to him. In due course MacLean found a second and longer account in an open letter from Father Brown of the Oxford mission, put on the children's page of the July 1922 mission magazine. This also attributed the rescue to villagers and came from Singh (MacLean 1977: 239). The Reverend was clearly responsible for disseminating two different stories of the discovery. He may have had legitimate reasons but clearly he provided two conflicting stories about the girls' discovery.

## The story discredited

William Ogburn and Nirmal Bose conducted an investigation in the early 1950s. They sought the site of the original discovery and any surviving witnesses who saw the girls behaving abnormally. From a discussion with Singh's daughter they concluded that Singh was probably familiar with other stories of wolf children. Louise Mani Das, a resident at the orphanage from 1932, said that most of the book was not true and that her uncle, Bhagabat Khatua, brought the children to Singh (Ogburn and Bose 1959: 149). Chandrakunda Das confirmed that his brother in law had rescued the children without any reference to a wolf's den.

Two superintendents said that the villages, Godamuri and Tpuban, mentioned by Singh did not exist. Ogburn and Bose also noted that there were no records of the girls' deaths although photographs of Kamala existed and several witnesses saw the girls at the orphanage. The failure to find Godamuri appeared to provide a conclusive indication of Singh's dishonesty. Yet the girls had been at the orphanage and their behaviour remained unexplained.

## MacLean's investigation

As Charles MacLean conducted his own research in the 1970s he found that nobody in the area remembered Ogburn and Bose visiting. Dr Jyotima Sarma, a sociologist who once studied under Ogburn in Chicago, said that he came to India in 1951 but was too old for active fieldwork (MacLean 1977: 297–8). According to her Bose took over the research. Bose was a known nationalist while Singh had been a republican who disowned his son for attending one of Gandhi's meetings in 1925. Sarma implied that most of the work was done by students and that Bose had intended to discredit Singh.

MacLean said that one of Singh's daughters showed him a portion of the original diary manuscript. The rest had been consumed by white ants. Crucially he found Godamuri which had changed its name to Ghorabandha. He confirmed that Chunarem had lived there and found one old man, Lasa Marandi, who claimed to have taken part in the original hunt as a boy of sixteen. Marandi testified that Singh, whom he described clearly, along with two Europeans and an Indian, Dibakar Bhanji Deo, had been present.

If Lasa Marandi's evidence is accepted then Singh is exonerated and we do have an authenticated case of children being found in a wolf's den. However the word of one witness cannot be accepted five decades after the event and the word of another who put out a contradictory story cannot be taken either. The researches of Ogburn, Bose and MacLean have made the case more intriguing. They have not proved or disproved Singh's original assertion that he found Kamala and Amala in a wolf's den under a termite mound.

## Further newspaper reports

On 5 April 1927 *The Times* reported the discovery of a wolf-child in Allahabad. He was found by herdsmen near Miswana. Two days later the newspaper published a letter from Lionel James in Berkshire who said that an Indian friend had seen a male wolf-child, recaptured at the age of seven. The friend's theory was that the child was taken as food but got mixed in the she-wolf's litter. Another letter, also published on 7 April 1927, from Osmond Reedy said that two Moslems used to tour Bihar with a wolf-girl.

A further wolf child was reported in Allahabad in 1926 and was reported in *The Daily Mail* on 26 April that year as a proven case. The evidence mentioned consisted of the child's preference for raw meat and roots, the discovery of his footprints among paw marks, a mauling on his face, that he barked instead of spoke, and was discovered in a wolf's cave. The boy was seven years old and apparently received medical treatment at Allahabad. The article also specifies that no suggestion of suckling was made and stated that it is not implausible for wolves to look after children as dogs can do this.

A wolf is unlikely to successfully suckle a human child as the milk would provide insufficient nourishment although the *Mumbai Mirror* reported a boy who had become accustomed to dog's milk in an article published on 15 April 2006. Unlike the classical myths, none of the Indian wolf boy stories describe suckling of children. Instead they feature older children without a suggestion that the wolf weaned them. Children or adults could quite plausibly live with wolves. Recent television documentaries have featured people living with gorillas and wild dogs, and even scientists who have lived with wolves, although not for a considerable length of time.

However children found with a wolf pack need not necessarily be members of that pack. Although mostly unconfirmed, the various reports in this chapter about children found in the company of wolves share key facts. They are all from areas where children were frequently exposed and where they may not have been taught to fear animals. Amid all the chicanery and rumour there once existed two very unusual girls in Midnapore. The absence of verification does not affect the belief in wolves rearing children.

## Wolf boys in fiction

Perhaps the most famous wolf-child is Rudyard Kipling's Mowgli. *The Jungle Book* (Kipling 1894) contributed to the mythology surrounding man-eating tigers in the West, although its portrayal of friendly gregarious wolves, four decades before Adolph Murie's work in Alaska, was not widely accepted. In writing his collection of short stories about Mowgli, Kipling may well have been influenced by his father's book *Beast and Man in India* (Kipling 1891) which referred to some wolf boy stories.

*The Jungle Book* was made into an animated film by Disney in 1967. Focusing on the friendship between Mowgli, the bear Baloo and the panther Baghera, this was very successful.

An Australian, Andrew Ward, runs a website on feral children at www.feralchildren.com. This is the starting point for all serious researchers. It contains summaries of all the major cases and links to other interesting sites.

### Contemporary opinions on wolf-children

Question seventeen of the survey asked if it was possible for children to be raised by wolves. 181 respondents answered this question and their answers are given below.

| Answer | Replies |
|--------|---------|
| Yes | 92 |
| No | 66 |
| Possibly | 22 |

Despite the absence of reliable evidence the majority of the respondents felt that it was possible for wolves to raise children. It isn't clear what sources influenced this perception. *The Jungle Book,* including the Disney version, is a possibility as are recent newspaper reports of modern wolf children. The *Daily Star's* cover on 01 September 1990 featured a Bangladeshi wolf-boy whose hirsute condition was apparently caused by a hormone deficiency. Singh's discovery of the wolf girls and the accounts of the British officials in India were circulated in England at the time but are not well-known now.

The topic continues to fascinate people but no firm evidence that wolves raised children has ever been found. Nor has the belief in wolves eating people been confirmed. Research into the reasons why people believe in these occurrences may prove more productive than searching for verification of individual cases. Understanding the reasons behind the beliefs about wolves is vital in the context of contemporary plans to reintroduce wolves to areas where they once existed, including parts of Great Britain.

# Chapter seven

# Contemporary beliefs about wolves

The results of the survey indicate that many of the respondents had a limited knowledge about wolves. Their answers were more likely to be influenced by fiction and films as opposed to the studies of zoologists. Current plans to reintroduce wolves all require an element of educating local people about wolves.

## The reintroduction of wolves

The reintroduction of wolves to the United Kingdom, specifically the Highlands of Scotland, has been suggested on more than one occasion. If this occurred it would not be without precedent. Beavers, wild boar, dormice and red kite have all returned to the UK, not always with government approval. The American states of Arizona, Wyoming, Idaho and Montana have all reintroduced wolves in specific areas. Wolves have also re-established populations in Scandinavia and other parts of Europe.

On 12 September 2006 the *Daily Telegraph* reported that a group called the Wild Beasts Trust was planning to release packs of wolves and lynx in Northumberland. This would be illegal as reintroduced species have to be licensed by the Department for the Environment, Food and Rural Affairs. Other groups that support reintroduction are following the legal process.

In 2004 a millionaire named Pat Lister outlined plans to reintroduce wolves, bison, lynx, bear and boar to his 23,000 acre estate. Another landowner, Paul van Vlissingen, has offered a further 81,000 acres to the scheme. Mr van Vlissingen commissioned a three-year study in 2005 on deer and their impact on the land. He believes that wolves are needed to control the deer population in the area.

## Arguments in favour of reintroducing wolves

The Wolf Trust based in Reading has published a manifesto aimed at reviving the Highlands, supporting the reintroduction of bear and lynx as well as wolves (Wolf Specialist Group 2002). They argue that the British Government should consider reintroducing wolves because it signed the Berne Convention on the Conservation of European Wildlife and Natural Habitats in 1979 and the European Union Council Directive 92/43/EEC on the Conservation of Natural Habitats and of Wild Fauna and Flora in 1992. The former has a recommendation that governments in areas where wolves are extinct should support conservation by promoting public awareness, encouraging research, studying reintroduction possibilities and collaborating with states where wolves survive. Article 22 of the 1992 Habitats Directive also recommends this.

The other main argument in favour of reintroducing wolves is economic. This is somewhat ironic since economic reasons undoubtedly led to the extinction of wolves in many European countries, possibly including England. The situation has changed because of the increase in tourism. At present thousands of English people go abroad to watch wildlife in their natural surroundings. There are companies specifically selling wolf tours to Slovakia, Russia, Ukraine and Canada. If wolves were in Scotland then it is likely that tourists from England and elsewhere would go there, helping boost the fragile Highland economy.

The Wolf Trust state that high numbers of deer in the Highlands are causing ecological problems and that the wolf is their natural predator. Only two of the six species of deer in Britain are native, the other four having been introduced by humans. Despite this, the reintroduction of wolves is considered unreasonable by many people.

### Arguments against reintroducing wolves

The principal arguments against reintroducing wolves to the Highlands are the perceived danger to people and the impact on livestock. Experiences in other countries show that wolf predation on livestock is minimal and manageable when the government compensates farmers for those losses. A similar scheme of compensation would have to operate in Scotland, and the costs considered. Although deer are abundant, wolves would also prey on sheep.

A bigger obstacle is public opinion. The Wolf Trust acknowledges that wolves can only be reintroduced when broad public opinion supports this. In a survey carried out by Scotland's rural gateway between August and September 2006, 24 of 34 respondents favoured the reintroduction of wolves (Rural Community Gateway 2005). Of course this is not fully representative and opposition can be expected from farmers as well as parents of young children. Educating them is essential if any reintroduction is to be successful.

### Contemporary attitudes towards reintroduction

Question twelve of the survey asked if wolves should be allowed to live in areas where there is a high human population. Of course any reintroduction of wolves would take place in a sparsely populated area but the answers give an indication of how favourably reintroduction proposals might be accepted.

Of the 175 respondents who answered this question, 57 felt that wolves should be allowed to live in these areas and 93 felt that they should not. The remainder were undecided.

*Kiri and Socrates play in snow at Wolf Park, Indiana. Photograph by Monty Sloan, www.wolfphotography.com, reproduced with kind permission of the photographer whose website contains many other professional photographs of wolves. Monty is associated with Wolf Park in Indiana, a non-profitmaking educational and research facility, established in 1972.*

### Education about wolves

The best way to educate people about wolves is by providing opportunities to see them. Sadly this is not possible and, although television documentaries may influence some, there will also be those who believe that the wolf in Little Red Riding Hood is representative of the species as a whole. Better education is required, not going to the erroneous extremes of portraying wolves as cuddly creatures and suitable as pets, but emphasising that their predatory nature almost certainly does not extend to people.

Wolves are not able to tell their own tale and arguably no human is qualified to undertake the role either. In Canada rangers mimic wolf calls and tourists gather to hear a reply. But the howling is no longer perceived as a threat as they listen to the elusive animals. They will remain elusive because the web of fear spun by our ancestors has not dissipated. Sheep and the livelihoods of their owners are still threatened. The dense untamed forests have largely been eradicated but the wolf is returning to some of his former territory and encountering a degree of tolerance.

Wolves live on, in the mind and in the wilderness where self-proclaimed 'civilised' people no longer perceive them as an enemy but as an inferior animal to be preserved. The history of wolves is closely interwoven with that of humans. The true story may not feature ravenous beasts attacking travellers, eating children thrown from sledges, or transforming into men under a full moon. Nonetheless the survival of beliefs that cannot be substantiated directly threatens wolves today. While the work of scientists has challenged traditional assumptions about wolves, it has been slow to change popular beliefs. Linnell's report and the studies by Mech and Murie are not widely known. The elimination of surviving inaccuracies is required although there are indications that the current generation in England view wolves more favourably than their predecessors.

# Bibliography

**Anonymous**

Anon., circa 1450, *Journal d'Un Borgeois de Paris*, translated by J. Shipley as *A Parisian Journal 1405–1449*, Clarendon, 1958.

Anon., 1590, *A True Discourse, declaring the damnable life and death of one Stubbe Peter, a most wicked sorcerer, who in the likeness of a woolfe, committed many murders, continuing this devilish practice 25 years, killing and devouring men, women and children, who, for the same fact was broken and executed the 31 October last past in the town of Bedbur near the city of Cologne, truly translated out of the High Dutch according to copie printed in Cologne, brought into England by George Bore*, Edward Venge.

Anon., 1673, *A Magicial Vision or a prefect discovery of the fallacies of witchcraft as it was lately represented in a pleasant sweet dream to a holy sweet sister, a faithful and precious assertor of the family of the Stand-hups, for preservation of the saints, from being tainted with the heresies of the congregations of the Doe-Littles*, Thomas Palmer.

Anon., 1799, *The Child's new Spelling Primer, or, First Book for Children. To which is added the stories of Cinderilla and the Little Red Riding Hood*, T. Wilkinson.

Anon., 1808, *The History of Red Riding Hood in Verse*, B Tabart.

Anon., 1834, *Little Red Riding Hood*, William W. Weekes.

Anon., 1933, 'The European Wolf', *Nature*, 09 December 1933, 906.

Adams, Francis, 1847, *The Seven Books of Paulus Aegineta*, 3 Volumes, Sydenham Society.

Adams, Harriet Isabel, 1893, *Little Red Riding Hood and the History of Tom Thumb. Illustrated by H.I. Adams*, Banbury Cross Series.

Aelian, Claudius, 1953, *On the Characteristics of Animals*, 3 Volumes, translated by A.F. Scholfield, Loeb Library.

Aesop, 1988, *The Complete Fables*, translated O. and R. Temple, Penguin.

Aiken, Joan, 1992, *The Wolves of Willoughby Chase*, Random House.

Albert the Great, 1987, *Man and the Beasts, de Animalibus. Books 22–26.*, translated by J.J. Scanlan, Medieval and Renaissance Centre and Studies.

Alliance for the Wild Rockies, 2006, 'Put it in perspective', downloaded May 2006 from www.wildrockiesalliance.org/issues/wolves/articles/perspective.html

Andrew, of Wyntoun, 1903, *The Original Chronicle of Andrew of Wyntoun.* Edited with introduction, notes and glossary by F.J. Armours. 2 Volumes, Scottish Text Society.

Aristotle, 1938, *Parts of Animals*, translated by A I. Peck, Loeb Library.

Aristotle, 1943, *Generation of Animals*, translated by A.I. Peck, Loeb Library.

Aristotle, 1991, *Historia Animalium*, translated by A.I. Peck and D M. Balme, Loeb Library.

Arnold, Thomas, 1890, *Annals and Memorials of St Edmund's Abbey*, Rolls Series.

Augustine, 1984, *City of God*, translated H. Bettenson, Penguin.

Bacchilega, Cristina, 1997, *Postmodern Fairy Tales, Gender and Narrative Strategies*, University of Pennsylvania Press.

Ball, Valentine, 1880, *Jungle Life in India*, T. de la Rue and Co.

Barber, Richard, 1992, *Bestiary, being an English version of the Bodleian Library, Oxford M.S. Bodley 764*, Folio Society.

Baring-Gould, Sabine, 1865, *The Book of Werewolves*, Smith and Elder.

Bayfield, Robert, 1633, *A Treatise de morborum capitis essentiis & prognostics.* D. Maxwell.

Beckford, Peter, 1798, *Thoughts on Hunting*, D. Bremmer.

Bede, 1991, *Ecclesiastical History of the English Church and People*, translated by L. Sherley Price, revised by R. Latham, Penguin.

Beer, Jeanette, 1986, *Master Richard's Bestiary of Love and Response*, University of California Press.

Bernard, Richard, 1627, *A Guide to Grand Jurymen*, Ed. Blackmore.

Berners, Juliana, 1880, *A treatyse on Fysshynge with an angle... Being a facsimile reproduction of the first book on the subject of fishing in England by Wynkyn de Worde in 1496.* With an introduction by Rev M.G. Watkins.

Bettleheim, Bruno, 1967, *The Empty Fortress*, Free Press.

Boethius, 1978, *The Consolation of Philosophy,* translated S.H. Tester, Loeb Library.

Boguet, Henry, 1929, *An Examen of Witches,* translated E. Allen-Ashwin, edited M. Summers, John Rodker.

Bishop, Norman, A., 1998, 'Child lifting by a wolf in India', *International Wolf,* Winter 1998, 17–18.

Blaine, Delabere, 1800, *An Encyclopaedia of Rural Sports; or, a Complete account, historical, practical and descriptive, of hunting, shooting, fishing, racing and other field sports and athletic amusements of the present day,* Longmans and Co, reprinted 1852.

Brewer, Ebenzer Cobhan, 1993, *Dictionary of Phrase and Fable*, Wordsworth.

Briggs, Robin, 1996, *Witches and Neighbours*, HarperCollins.

Britton, Paul, 2001, *Picking up the Pieces*, Corgi.

Burgess, Glyn S., and Keith Busby, 1986, *The Lais of Marie de France*, Penguin.

Cambrensis, Giraldus, 1867, *Opera*, translated J.F. Dimock, Rolls Series.

Carbyn, Lu, 1989, 'Coyote attacks on children in western North-America', *Wildlife Society Bulletin*, 17, 4, 444–6.

Carter, Angela, 1979, *The Bloody Chamber and Other Stories*, Gollancz.

Carter, Angela, 1995, *Burning Your Boats: Collected Short Stories,* Chatto and Windus.

Caxton, William, 1984, *The History of Reynard the Fox*, edited by N.F. Blake, Oxford University Press.

Cohn, Norman, 1970, 'The myth of Satan and his human servants'. In M.R Douglas (ed), *Witchcraft Confessions and Accusations*, Tavistock Publications.

Corbett, Jim, 1954, *The Man-Eating Leopard of Rudraprayag*, Oxford University Press.

Crane, Walter, 1875, *The Blue Beard Picture Book, Containing Blue Beard, Little Red Riding Hood, Jack and the Bean-Stalk, Baby's own ABC.* G. Routledge and Sons.

Dahl, Roald, 1982, *Revolting Rhymes,* Puffin.

*Dante, 1984, Divine Comedy,* translated by N. Muss, Penguin.

Davies, Edward, 1875, *Wolf Hunting in Brittany*, Chapman and Hall.

Dent, Anthony, 1974, *Lost Beasts of Britain*, Harrap.

Douglas, David C, and George W Greenway, 1961, *English Historical Documents* Volume 2, Eyre Methuen.

Edward, Duke of York, 1909, *The Master of Game*, edited by William A. and Florence N. Baillie-Grohman, Hanson and Co.

Eisler, Robert, 1959, *Man Into Wolf,* Routledge and Kegan Paul.

Endores, Guy, 1963, *The Werewolf of Paris,* Panther.

Flemming, Alexander, 1577, *A Strange and Terrible Wunder...* Francis Goudley.

Florus, Publius Annius, 1669, translated John Davies, *The Roman History of L.J.F made English*, Samuel Snead.

Fraser, Mark, 2003, 'Wolf' (quoting anonymous source in *Bridport and Lyme Regis News* 29 Aug 2003), www.beastwatch.co.uk/Dorset.htm#WOLF; downloaded 29 October 2006.

Frazer, James George, 1993, *The Golden Bough*, Wordsworth.

Fritts, Stephen H, 1983, 'Record dispersal by a wolf from Minnesota', *Journal of Mammalogy* 64, 166–7.

Gerstein, Mary, 1974, 'Germanic Warg, the Outlaw as Werewolf', In G. Larson (ed), *Myth in Indo-European Antiquity*, University of California Press.

Goulart, Simon, 1607, *Admirable and Memorable Histories*, translated E. Grimeston, George Elder.

Gregory of Tours, 1927, *The History of the* Franks, translated by O.M. Dalton, 2 Volumes, Clarendon Press.

Grimm, Jacob and Wilhelm Grimm, 1924, *Fairy Tales*, translated E. Taylor, C. Baldwin.

Harpur, Merrily, 2006, *Mystery Big Cats*, Heart of Albion.

Harting, James, 1994, *A Short History of the Wolf in Britain,* Pryor Publications.

Herlihy, David, 1971, *The History of Feudalism*, Macmillan.

Herodotus, 1996, *The Histories*, translated by G. Rawlinson, Wordsworth.

Hill, John, 1752, *A General Natural History*, 3 Volumes, Thomas Osborne.

Holtgen, Karl Joseph, 'Why are there no wolves in England?', *Anglia*, 99, 60–82.

Horwood, Alfred J., 1866, *Yearbook of the Reign of Edward 1, 1292, 20 and 21*, Rolls Series.

Ireland, William W., 1900, *The Mental Afflictions of Children*, J A Churchill.

James I, 1597, *Demonologie in forme of a dialogue*, Robert Walgrave.

Jamsedji, Jivania, 1880, *Astrodan and Recorded Instances of Children Having Been Nurtured by Wolves,* Education Society Press.

Jones, Malcolm, 2002, 'The Lambe Speaketh.... An addendum', *Journal of the Warburg and Courtauld Institute*, 63, 287–94.

Keynes, Simon and Michael Lapidge, 1983, *Alfred the Great, Asser's Life of King Alfred and Other Contemporary Sources*, Penguin.

Kipling, John Lockwood, 1891, *Beast and Man in India*, Macmillan.

Kipling, Rudyard, 1894, *The Jungle Book*, Century.

Kolenosky, George B., 1972, 'Hybridization between wolf and coyote', *Journal of Mammalogy*, 52: 446–9.

Kramer, Heinrich and Sprenger, Jakob, 1971, *Malleus Maleficarum*, translated E. Allen-Ashwin, edited M. Summers, Arrow.

Lane, Harlan, 1971, *The Wild Boy of Aveyron,* Allen and Urwin.

L'Estragne, Roger, 1692, *Fables of Aesop,* R. Sare.

Leibnitz, Gottfried Wilhelm, 1710, *Scriptores Rerum Brunvicensium*, Nicolai Sumtis.

Lessing, Theodore, 1993, *Monsters of the Weimar*, Nemesis Publications.

Lewis, Clive Staples, 1950, *The Lion, the Witch and the Wardrobe*, Geoffrey Bles.

Lindskog, Berger, 1954, *African Leopard Men*, Studia Ethnograpgica Upsalliensia.

Linnell John., Reidar Andersen, Zanete Andersone, Linas Balciauskas, Juan Carlos Blanco, Luigi Boitani, Scott Brainerd, Urs Breitenmoser, Ilpo Kojola, Olof Liberg, Jonny Loe, Henryk Okaram, Hans C Pedersen, Christoph Promberger, Hakan Sand H, Erling J Solberg, Harri Valdmann and Petter Wabakken , 2002, *The Fear of Wolves: a Review of Wolf Attacks on Humans,* Norwegian Institute for Natural Research.

London, Jack, 1903, *The Call of the Wild*, Macmillan,

London, Jack, 1906, *White Fang*, Macmillan,

Lopez, Barry, 1978, *Of Wolves and Men*, J.M. Dent.

Lydekker, Richard, 1894, *Royal Natural History*, Frederick Warne.

McCarthy, E., 1924, 'Greek and Roman lore of animal-nursed Infants', *Michigan Academy of Science, Arts and Letters*, 4.1, 15–24.

MacIntyre, Rick, 1995, *War Against the Wolf*, Voyageur.

MacLean, Charles, 1977, *The Wolf Children*, Allen Lane.

Magnus, Olaus, 1658, *A Compendious History of the Goths, Swedes and Vandals and other Northern Nations*, J. Streater.

Malory, Thomas, 1485, *La Morte D'Arthur*, reprinted Ware 1996.

Manwood, John, 1615, *A Treatise of the Lawes of the Forest*, Company of Stationers.

Marchant, Guy, 1493, *The Kalendar and Compost of Shepherds,* reprinted Peter Davies 1930.

Marshall, John, 1823, *Marshall's Edition of the Popular Story of Little Red Riding Hood,* John Marshall, 1823.

Mech, David, 1962, *The Wolves of Isle Royale*, US Government Prints Service, Fauna Series 7.

Mech, David, 1970, *The Wolf: the Ecology and Behaviour of an Endangered Species,* Natural History Press.

Meredith, Stephen, 2003, 'Wolves spotted in a villager's garden', *News and Star* 20 Nov 2003; online ar www.beastwatch.co.uk/Cumbria.html; downloaded 29 October 2006.

Milne, F.A., 1904, 'Arthur and Gorlagon', *Folklore*, 15, 40–67.

Mowat, Farley, 1979, *Never Cry Wolf*, Pan.

Murray, Margaret, 1921, *The Witch-Cult in Western Europe*, Clarendon.

Murray, Margaret, 1970, *The God of the Witches*, Oxford University Press.

Murie, Adolph, 1944, *The Wolves of Mount McKinley,* US National Park Service Fauna Series 5.

Nash, Roderick, 1967, *Wilderness and the American Mind*, Yale University Press, reprinted 1970.

NDTV Correspondent, 2001, Man-eating wolf kills girl in UP village, www.ndtv.com/morenews/showmorestory.asp?id=16843; downloaded October 2003.

Nelson, Janet, 1991, *The Annals of St Bertin*, Manchester University Press.

Oates, Caroline F, 1993, *Trials of Werewolves in the Franche-Comte in the Early Modern Period*, Unpublished University of London PhD thesis.

Ogburn, William and Bose, Nirmal, 1959, 'On the Trail of the Wolf Children', *Genetic Psychology Monographs,* 60, 117–93.

Oldfather, Charles Henry, 1933, *Diodorus of Sicily,* Loeb.

Otten, Charlotte, 1986, *A Lycanthropy Reader*, Syracuse University Press.

Ovid, 1986, *Metamorphoses*, translated A.D. Melville, Oxford University Press.

Paul, Bill, Carter Niemeyer, Ed Bangs and Elizabeth Harper, 2004, *Depredation on Livestock and Pets*, downloaded May 2006 from www.wolf.org/wolves/learn/intermed/inter_mgmt/depred_livestock.asp

Pausanias, 1979, *Guide to Greece*, translated P. Levi, 2 Volumes, Penguin.

Perrault, Charles, 1725, *Histories or Tales of Past Times*, translated C. Pote, R. Samber.

Perry, Ben, 1965, *Babrius and Phaedrus,* Loeb Library.

Petronius, 1959, *Satyricon*, translated W. Arrowsmith, University of Michigan Press.

Plato, 1940, *Republic,* translated F. Mac Donald Cornford, Clarendon.

Pleasants, Craig, 1994, *The Three Little Pigs as it was originally passed into English folklore in 1620*, Gate of Heck.

Pliny the Elder, 1960, *Natural History*, 10 Volumes, translated H. Rackman, Loeb Library.

Pollard, John, 1964, *Wolves and Werewolves,* Hale.

Poole, Joshua, 1657, *The English Parnassus*, Thomas Johnson.

Procopius, 1914, *The History of the Wars*, 6 Volumes, translated H. B. Dewing, Heinemann.

Pullainen, Erkki, 1979, 'Ecology of the Wolf in the Settled Areas of Finland', in *The Behavior and Ecology of Wolves, Proceedings of the Symposium on the Behavior and Ecology of Wolves*, edited by Erich Klinghammer, Garland STPM Press.

Rawcliffe, Carol, 1997, *Medicine and Society in Later Medieval England*, Sutton Publishing.

Redfern, Nick, 'The Werewolves of Britain', *Fate*, March 2006, downloaded May

2006 from www.fatemag.com/issues/2000s/2006-03article1a.html

Reid, George W., 1870, *Catalogue of Prints and Drawings in the British Museum.* Division 1. Political and Personal Satires (Catalogue of political and personal satires etc), British Museum.

Remy, Nicholas, 1930, *Demonolatry,* translated E. Allen-Ashwin, edited M. Summers, John Rodker.

Reuter, Timothy, 1992, *The Annals of Fulda,* Manchester University Press.

Route, Bill and Linda Aylsworth, 1999, *1999 World Wolf Status Report,* downloaded May 2006 from www.wolf.org/wolves/learn/basic/populations/fall99insert.asp

Rural Community Gateway, 2005, 'Re-introduction of Lynx and Wolves? Rural Gateway Survey Results', www.ruralgateway.org.uk/cgi-bin/library.cgi?action=detail&id=1199&dir_publisher_varid=1; downloaded downloaded 22 October 2006.

Sawyer, Peter, 1962, *The Age of the Vikings,* Edward Arnold.

Reynolds, George, 1975, *Wagner the Wehr-Wolf,* edited E.F. Bleiler, Constable.

Scott, Martin, 1960, *The Heliand,* University of North Carolina.

Scott, Reginald, 1886, *The Discoverie of Witchcraft,* Elliot Stock.

Scribner, Robert W, 1994, *For the Sake of Simple Folk,* Clarendon.

Seton, Ernest Thompson, 1937, *Mainly About Wolves,* Methuen.

Skeat, William W., 1867a, *Pierce the Ploughman's Crede,* Early English Text Society.

Skeat, William W., 1867b, *The Romance of William of Palerne,* Early English Text Society.

Sleeman, William Henry, 1852, *An Account of Wolves nurturing Children in their Dens,* Jenkin Thomas.

Sleeman, William Henry, 1971, *Sleeman in Oudh: An abridgment of W.H. Sleeman's 'A journey through the Kingdom of Oudh in 1849–50',* edited with an introduction and notes by P.D. Reeves, Cambridge University Press.

Smith, Mervyn, A., 1904, *Sport and Adventure in the Indian Jungle,* Hurst and Blackett.

Smith, William George, 1948, *The Oxford Dictionary of English Proverbs,* Clarendon.

Stewart, Caroline T., 1909, 'The Origin of the Werewolf Superstition', in G.W. Brown, edited, *University of Missouri Studies, Volume 2, Social Sciences,* University of Missouri, 269–93.

Stevenson, Robert Louis, 1879, *Travels with a Donkey,* reprinted Blackie 1965.

Stone, Alby, 1994, 'Hellhounds, werewolves and the Germanic underworld', *Mercian Mysteries,* 20.

Storr, Catherine, 1982, *Clever Polly and the Stupid Wolf,* Chivers Press.

Storr, Catherine, 1985, *Tales of Polly and the Hungry Wolf,* Chivers Press.

Storr, Catherine, 1990, *Last Stories of Polly and the Wolf,* Chivers Press.

Summers, Montague, 1933, *The Werewolf,* Kegan Paul.

Summers, Montague, 1973, *The History of Witchcraft and Demonology,* Routledge and Kegan Paul.

Swan, Charles, 1877, *Gesta Romanorum,* G. Bell.

Swanton, Michael, 1998, *The Anglo-Saxon Chronicle,* Routledge.

Thomas, Arthur Hermann, *Calendar of Early Mayor's Court Rolls of the City of London,* Cambridge University Press, 1925.

Thompson, Richard H., 1991, *Wolf Hunting in France in the Reign of Louis XV, the Beast of the Gevuadan,* Edwin Mellen.

Thompson, Sith, 1966, *Motif-Index of Folk Literature,* 6 Volumes, Indiana University Press.

Thorpe, Benjamen, 1840, *Ancient Laws and Institutes of England,* Eyre and Spottiswoode.

Thorpe, Benjamen, 1857, *The Life of King Alfred the Great,* H.G. Bonn.

Thornhill, Mark, 1899, *Haunts and Hobbies of an Indian Official,* London, J. Murray.

Tolkien, John Ronald Reuel, 1937, *The Hobbit,* G. Allen and Unwin.

Turbeville, George, 1576, *Turbeville's Book of Hunting,* reprinted Clarendon 1908.

Turton, William, 1820, *A General System of Nature through the Three Grand Kingdoms of Animals, Vegetables and Minerals,* 7 Volumes, Lackington and Allen.

Tylor, Edward B., 1871, *Primitive Culture,* 2 Volumes, reprinted Harper 1958.

Verstegan, R., 1605, *Restitution of Decayed Intelligence in Antiquities, concerning the most noble and renowned English Nation*, Robert Braines.

Walpole, Horace, 1820, *Correspondence of Horace Walpole*, 4 Volumes, Rodwell and Martin.

Webster, John, 2003, *The Duchess of Malfi*, Longman.

Weisse, Thomas F., William L Robinson, Richard A Hook and L. David Mech, 1979, 'An Experimental Translocation of the Eastern Timber Wolf', in Erik Klinghammer edited *The Behavior and Ecology of Wolves, Proceedings of the Symposium on the Behavior and Ecology of Wolves*, Garland SPTM Press.

Whelan, William, 1860, *History and Topography of the Counties of Cumberland and Westmoreland*, White and Co.

William of Malmesbury, *circa* 1128, *Chronicles of the Kings of England,* edited by J. A. Giles, Bell and Son, 1883.

William of Newburgh, 1856, *The History of William of Newburgh translated from the Latin by Joseph Stevenson*, Seeleys.

Williams, Paul. 2003, *Cultural Impressions of the wolf, with specific reference to the man-eating wolf in England*, Unpublished PhD thesis, University of Sheffield.

Whitelock, Dorothy, 1955, *English Historical Documents*, Eyre Methuen.

Wood Rendell, Alan, 1928, *Physiologus, A metrical Bestiary of Twelve Chapters by Bishop Theobald, Printed in Cologne, 1492*, John Edwin.

Wolf Specialist Group, 2002, 'Manifesto: Declaration of Principles for Wolf Conservation', www.wolftrust.org.uk/index.html; downloaded 22/10/2006.

Wright, Aaron E., 1997, *The Fables of Walter of England*, Pontificial Institute of Mediaeval Studies.

Wright, Thomas, 1839, *The Political Songs of England from the Reign of John to that of Edward II*, Camden.

Ziolkowski, Jan M, 1992, 'A Fairy Tale from before Fairy Tales: Egbert of Liege's 'De peulla a lupellis servata and the Medieval Background of 'Little Red Riding Hood', *Speculum, 67, 549–75*.

Zimen, Erik, 1980, *The Wolf, his Place in the Natural World*, Souvenir Press.

Zimen, Erik., and Luigi Boitani, 1979, 'Status of the wolf in Europe and the possiblities of conservation and reintroduction' in E. Klinghammer (ed), *The Behavior and Ecology of Wolves: Proceedings of the Symposium on the Behavior and Ecology of Wolves*, Garland SPTM Press, 43–83.

Zipes, Jack, 1988, *The Brothers Grimm, From Enchanted Forests to the Modern World*, Routledge.

Zipes, Jack, 1993, *The Trials and Tribulations of Little Red Riding Hood,* Routledge.

# INDEX

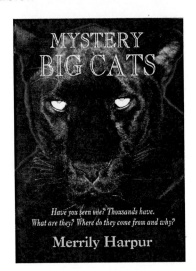

# Mystery Big Cats

## Merrily Harpur

In the past twenty years every county in Britain, from Caithness to Cornwall, has had recurrent sightings of 'big cats' – described as being like pumas or panthers. These anomalous big cats sightings are now running at an estimated 1,200 a year.

Farmers, gamekeepers, ornithologists, policemen and even parents on the school run have all been thrilled – or terrified – to see what they assume is a big cat escaped from a zoo. Yet these big cats are neither escapees from zoos nor, as this book conclusively argues, the descendants of pets released into the countryside by their owners in 1976 when the Dangerous Wild Animals Act made it too expensive to keep big cats.

The questions therefore remain, what are they and where have they come from? With the orthodox explanations overturned, Merrily Harpur searches for clues in the cultures of other times and places. She discovers our mystery felines have been with us for longer than we imagine, and throws unexpected light on the way Western civilisation looks at the world.

*Mystery Big Cats* is the first serious and comprehensive book on the subject. From the drama of eyewitnesses' verbatim accounts to the excitement of new perspectives and insights into a strange and often terrifying experience – it gets to grips with what is now the commonest encounter with the unknown in Britain.

**Merrily Harpur** is a cartoonist and writer. She has published three books: *The Nightmares of Dream Topping, Unheard of Ambridge* and *Pig Overboard*. She divides her time between Dorset and Ireland, where she founded the Strokestown International Poetry Festival.

EAN 978 1872 883 922. Published 2006. 245 x 175 mm, 242 + viii pages, 55 b&w photographs, paperback. **£16.95**

# Explore Dragons

### Richard Freeman

The dragon is the most ancient and widespread of all monsters. Dragon legends are told in every culture and in every continent on Earth. Its breath condenses and forms rain in China. It slithers across the heavens in Mexico as Quetzalcoatl. In Scandinavian lore its coils encircled the whole earth. No other monster is so universal in its occurrence or so varied.

But the Britain Isles are the homeland of the dragon. Although a small country, it is seething with dragon legends. *Explore Dragons* puts British dragon stories into their international context and attempts to fathom out what really lurks behind these fanciful tales. Could dragons once have been real creatures? Are such creatures still alive?

**Richard Freeman** is a former zookeeper and has a degree in zoology. He is the zoological director of the Centre for Fortean Zoology in Exeter. A full-time cryptozoologist, he has searched for monsters and mystery animals in Indo-China, Sumatra, and Mongolia as well as in the UK.

ISBN 978 1 872883 939. Published 2006. Demy 8vo (215 x 138 mm), 187 + viii pages, 7 b&w photographs, 13 line drawings, paperback. **£12.95**

# Explore Phantom Black Dogs

## edited by Bob Trubshaw

Contributors: Jeremy Harte, Simon Sherwood, Alby Stone, Bob Trubshaw and Jennifer Westwood.

The folklore of phantom black dogs is known throughout the British Isles. From the Black Shuck of East Anglia to the Moody Dhoo of the Isle of Man there are tales of huge spectral hounds 'darker than the night sky' with eyes 'glowing red as burning coals'.

The phantom black dog of British and Irish folklore, which often forewarns of death, is part of a world-wide belief that dogs are sensitive to spirits and the approach of death, and keep watch over the dead and dying. North European and Scandinavian myths dating back to the Iron Age depict dogs as corpse eaters and the guardians of the roads to Hell. Medieval folklore includes a variety of 'Devil dogs' and spectral hounds. Above all, the way people have thought about such ghostly creatures has steadily evolved.

This book will appeal to all those interested in folklore, the paranormal and fortean phenomena.

> 'I think this must be the best entry in the Explore series I have seen so far... ' Aeronwy Dafies *Monomyth Supplement*

> 'This is an excellent work and is very highly recommended.' Michael Howard *The Cauldron*

ISBN 978 1 872883 786. Published 2005. Demy 8vo (215 x 138 mm), 152 + viii pages, 10 b&w half-tones, paperback. **£12.95**

# A Bestiary of Brass

## Peter Heseltine

From antelopes to wyverns, with over fifty species in between, *A Bestiary of Brass* looks the animals, birds, insects, fish – even shellfish – which have been depicted on medieval memorial brasses in Britain. Some are native, others – such as elephants and panthers – were exotic, while dragons and unicorns were as mythical then as they are today.

At the time they were engraved these creatures evoked a wide range of folklore and legends. This rich symbolism is brought to life by the author. But enigmas remain – why would anyone want to be associated with a fox when they were more noted for cunning and slyness, or a hedgehog, or even a whelk? We also find out about the lives of the people commemorated and share the author's detailed knowledge of their heraldic emblems. Practical advice is provided to help make brass rubbings and to learn more about these memorials.

The illustrations show a wide range of the memorials, with detailed views of the creatures they incorporate. *A Bestiary of Brass* will appeal to anyone interested in folklore, art and medieval history. Above all, these masterpieces of craftsmanship reveal that our deep fascination with animals was shared by our ancestors many hundreds of years ago.

ISBN 978 1 872 883 908. Published 2006. Demy 8vo (215 x 138 mm), over 280 illustrations, paperback . **£12.95**

# Heart of Albion

## The UK's leading publisher of folklore, mythology and cultural studies.

Further details of all Heart of Albion titles online at
**www.hoap.co.uk**

All titles available direct from Heart of Albion Press.

Please add 80p p&p (UK only; email
**albion@indigogroup.co.uk** for overseas postage).

To order books or request our current catalogue
please contact

**Heart of Albion Press**

2 Cross Hill Close, Wymeswold
Loughborough, LE12 6UJ

Phone: 01509 880725
Fax: 01509 881715
email: albion@indigogroup.co.uk
Web site: www.hoap.co.uk